# NOTEBOOKS
# 1970–2003

# NOTEBOOKS
# 1970–2003

## MURRAY BAIL

Harvill
*Secker*

Published by The Harvill Press 2005

2 4 6 8 10 9 7 5 3 1

Copyright © Murray Bail, 2005

First published in Great Britain and Australia in 2005 by
The Harvill Press
Random House, 20 Vauxhall Bridge Road,
London SWIV 2WA

Random House Australia (Pty) Limited
20 Alfred Street, Milsons Point, Sydney
New South Wales 2061, Australia

Random House New Zealand Limited
18 Poland Road, Glenfield
Auckland 10, New Zealand

Random House South Africa (Pty) Limited
Endulini, 5A Jubilee Road, Parktown 2193, South Africa

The Random House Group Limited Reg. No. 954009
www.randomhouse.co.uk/harvill

Bail, Murray, 1941–.
 Notebooks.
 ISBN 1 74051 353 3.

 1. Bail, Murray, 1941– – Notebooks, sketchbooks, etc.
 2. Authors, Australian – 20th century – Diaries. I. Title.

A828.303

A CIP catalogue record for this book is also available from the British
Library

Sections of this book have been previously published as
*Longhand: A Writer's Notebooks*, McPhee Gribble, 1989.

Cover design by Darian Causby/www.highway51.com.au
Typeset in 12 on 15 pt Apollo MT by Midland Typesetters, Australia
Printed and bound by Griffin Press, Netley, South Australia

ALSO PUBLISHED BY THE HARVILL PRESS

*Homesickness*
*Holden's Performance*
*Eucalyptus*

*The Drover's Wife and Other Stories*
*Camouflage*

*The Faber Book of Contemporary Australian Short
Stories* (editor)

NON-FICTION
*Ian Fairweather*

Six small notebooks, yellow with blue lettering 'SPIRAX No. 561', bought in Melbourne 1968 – the Indian and Afghanistan notebooks; one smaller with pink cover, bought in Bombay, now lost; eight shorthand notebooks, caramel covers, London 1970–74; one, used during the first American visit, 1972, lost. Entries here have been taken, with some corrections, mostly from seven 'London' books.

*London*
*June 1970–November 1974*

29.6.70. From Heathrow, in the red d/decker I felt myself swallowed by the flat maze of narrow passage-ways as it closed in behind, the reddish-brown brick, the blurred edges, grime and slate, and channelled in a roundabout way into the heart of the city, where I found there was no 'heart', no centre. A crowding-in quite different from Bombay and the other Indian cities. The architecture, the people going about their business, and – everywhere – advertisements displaying English words are related to me, though remote.

At the same time, seated upstairs with M. also silent, I felt 'above it all' and – adding to the illusion – not being British, not part of all this.

Vulnerability while stumbling with suitcases. So I assumed a stony expression.

England. What to call it? England? Or Britain? The UK? United Kingdom? Great Britain? The

British Isles? The words, words. Production of so many extra words here.

The necessity of shaking off pedantry, on my part.

After years in India: I feel a crowd of gazing bodies behind me.

Two women on footpath surveying each other severely. One had thick parallel legs, woollen stockings; the other was skinny, deeply lined.

1st: 'I was only saying to my husband, I should drop around. But I said, I don't even know her name.'

2nd: 'But we've known each other for years.'

1st: 'Yes, but I thought: should I just pop in?'

2nd: 'Of course you can. Pop around any time. It's number 27, by the station. Come and have a cup of tea, I'm always home. Your hem's undone.'

Story. 'Flat-hunting'. Begin: 'I felt flat so I went hunting . . .'

In each place the agent wearing the club tie simply gazed out of the window. The third-floor rooms behind Notting Hill station had everything removed except on the mantelpiece a page from a Sunday paper: '15 Ways to Tell a Thoroughbred Racehorse'. In W8, the shape of a crucifix outlined in nicotine on the wall; the back yard of the garden flat had rusty weight-lifting equipment lying in the weeds. (Instead of appraising each flat I found myself searching for traces of the previous tenants.)

Following M. into unknown buildings.

A West Indian filled the mailbag from the letter-box, dragged it into his van, and dropped a letter; at the same time a man delivering masses of fashion accessories from another van dropped a grey lizard belt and ran back for it. I looked from one to the other, then walked on.

Instead of laughing, he said, 'Ha, ha.'

Langham Street. Two rooms, basement. Looking up, I can see the ankles of English people.

Satisfaction: as if I wanted to live in uncomfortable conditions surrounded by rubbish bins. Not belonging here, I am against the majority.

A suitcase and a few books. I almost respect myself.

London's largest abortion clinic opposite. Its neon sign shines all night, and during the day the white-tiled façade, as in an institutional lavatory, reflects light into this underground room.

Neighbour on footpath speaking to woman on first floor:
'They only have foreign abortions, I read. Every nationality but English, those girls. It's a gold mine, I wouldn't mind having half. They had one of those ex . . . ex . . . ex . . . What do you call those things? Extractor fans. They put one of them right by my window. It was going all night. They must operate on those girls at night. I couldn't stand it. So the police came around there. "We might as well," they said. "Someone else threatened to put an explosion there."'

Taxis pull up and double-park. As if waiting to have their diesel pulse rate measured.

Punjabi in the fruit shop:
'How much will that be?'
'Six and nine only.'

Walking past the hospital I noticed two orderlies seated across a window-sill, knees raised, having a cup of tea. They were looking at the pedestrians, almost surprised by the verticality of normal people.

The light flow of music played by a trio of old men in overcoats, near Oxford Circus, seeking gaps between buildings.

Story: 'Encyclopedia' or 'Anthology'. List nouns, adjectives, verbs etc. which add up to define the existence of somebody. Definitions?

Bow-legged stall-holder in Berwick Street calling out at everybody, forcing smiles.

'You! Lady! You must have been beautiful a few years ago!'

Buck-teeth, chinless, forgetting his display of vegetables.

'Look at him not smiling! Look at him. Not a smile. What's the matter with him? What's happened to you all? Why doesn't anyone smile anymore? Look at that one.'

Distaste: not with myself, but him.

*What is a Comparison?*                    – Kitaj

Dog Museum (skulls etc.) – Vienna.
Bagpipe Museum in Newcastle-upon-Tyne.


Somewhere in the middle of America: A Barbed-Wire Museum.


At nights and weekends the streets are empty except for the old woman (the one wearing the powder-blue hat with veil) rummaging in the rubbish bins for off-cuts of material. On Sundays, burglar alarms ring for hours on end, which suggest a part of the city has been left deserted and burning.


At least the newspaper-seller with blackened hands can wipe the residue of the words off on his trousers.


I keep seeing people in pairs or singly consulting maps. Others are doing the crossword.


I knock on the door, someone opens it, looks at me, slams the door in my face. I am confronted with the grain and texture of wood, and bits of paint, a few inches away. There is a momentary illusion of what is 'real'.

Pleased with this new meaning of art – it should possess such a compelling force – I wrote to R.H. in Sydney, 'offering it'. A respectful but sober reply.

At first I pitied him (the bus conductor being abused by passengers); then I pitied him too much. I checked myself.

M.'s vagueness of speech when she is shy of someone (honesty). It makes me reconsider my own position.

Dog Show. Tiny, ancient woman goes to all the shows with her Pekinese 'to let him see what's going on. I never enter him, he just looks and enjoys himself'. And she kept asking officials for directions she didn't take. A committee-woman in tweed with flaming red-setter hair went about getting things done. When others were drawing a raffle, she was the one who said, 'You want the numbers called out?' She looked around like an auctioneer and bellowed briskly, 'NUMBER THIRTY-SIX!'

Crime is the Highest Form of Sensuality
— graffiti, Notting Hill

Along Oxford Street at night the rat kept running and stopping. I moved my foot slightly, but stopped. I imagined stamping on a rat to be an Oriental impulse. To preserve such a feeling I stood there for several seconds. The rat crossed the street in traffic, ran under moving cars, along the window of a store and down a side street. Two youths followed. Then I heard the sound of kicking.

At the meeting the pale, pudgy man by the window rattled the cup in the saucer. He used two hands to steady it. Concentrating, he became intent, entirely alone, as he shook and rattled and splashed — coffee on the carpet, his shoes.

Invent (for depth of individuality); less 'reportage'.

'In Cézanne's case, the artist triumphed over the male.'
— Françoise Lehel

I am at a job, but not only am I not working, I actively resist. I have drawn back, not wanting to be contaminated.

Narrow blue-veined face and grey hair erupting nautically around his ears which are suddenly like Henry Moore objects. He makes a practice of being judicious, especially of appearing judicious. 'It seems to me we could perhaps . . .' Or, 'I wonder if we could possibly . . .' The word 'fairly' is regularly chosen. Naturally he said to me, 'I don't think I can imagine the possibility of living somewhere else.'

Even in the cold, papers and other rubbish rolling along the currents of the footpath gave the street a hot appearance.

Outside the station a man playing the accordion with a photograph propped at his feet of himself as a young man in a crouching stance, EX-MIDDLEWEIGHT BOXER.

'Lying is the hint of morality.'                    – Conrad

Mother (mine) commenting on Adelaide suicide: 'Poor thing. She'd gone and had her hair permed the day before. It wasn't needed, was it?'

A way of thinking to be avoided:
'When an acquaintance greets me on the street by removing his hat, what I see from a formal point of view is nothing but a change of certain details within a configuration forming part of the general pattern of colour, lines and volumes, which constitute my world of vision.'
– Panofsky

Southampton. Irresistible desire to look between the boat and the wharf.

Hungry tourists. Hungry jaws, insistent necks. Dull Australians in hairy jackets mingling before getting aboard.

Empty pier, moist windows, listless seagulls: the usual melancholy of the seaside town out of season. How to avoid the truth of a cliché?

Sign on a building (cream-coloured): HAT, CAP AND HELMET FACTORY.

*Jenkin's Definition*. (Too English)

Landscape with dry grass (NSW) the colour of a doormat.


Running late, the carpenter phoned his wife. 'Hello, you all right?' His blunt affection. Like a familiar, leathery instrument.


This footpath and the universe.


Town called Perm (in Russia). Severely feminine.


Often says, 'I like it, I like it.'
    I think he's bluffing.


His passion for mushroom omelettes.


Scars on legs. 'Car accident,' he said.


The spread of central heating has broken the spell of the family circle around the fire, allowing each member to disperse to separate rooms and individualism.

Near Berkeley Square: THIS HOUSE WAS BUILT IN 1759.

So what?

Personal columns, *Sunday Times*:

KINGSTON MARKET, Friday 6th about 4 o'clock. You were walking, I was driving wearing red shirt, sunglasses. We smiled and passed. Please write Box AZ987.

Did he succeed? Repeating an intersection.


Today a young man double-parked his dented Morris outside the Langham Clinic to collect his girlfriend – did not have a married look. As she shuffled out somewhat dazed (small, not exactly neat figure, in a grey coat) he ran forward with his arm raised. I thought he would take the suitcase; but he motioned her to stand still, and stepping into the middle of the street, took her photograph, outside the abortion clinic. She appeared to face him, without lowering her luggage.

Inside, I noticed the day before, the large cigarette and coffee-making machines in the waiting room.


In the café, mid-afternoon, sliding shadow of double-decker flooded *everything*.

So, 'fellah' is Arabic!

But why do women walk, talk or stand — and enter restaurants — with their arms folded? Realising I'm frowning, I look away.

'Wherever the British Empire established itself, it introduced the game of billiards. It was typically and eccentrically British to popularise in far off places a game that required a weighty slab of slate measuring 12 feet by six feet to be carefully set on legs and covered with an immaculate stretch of the finest quality cloth. It says much for the quality of the game — or the tenacity of the billiard-table salesman in those days — that billiards was played keenly throughout the Empire and that tables appeared in tea plantations in Ceylon and India, the deserts of Libya, the Australian outback and in British military outposts all over the world, etc . . .'

Sir Thomas Phillipps (1792–1872) tried to own at least one copy of every book ever published.

It was possible then? Christie's is still auctioning them.

29th birthday. By 30, complete six stories, tighten entire novel (all over again). There is not enough reason for it at the moment (the novel).

'While the car owner was away, the chauffeur, who had a silver plate in his skull and was subject to blackouts, took all the servants out for a drive. On a bend he blacked out, and drove into a brick wall.'                    —*Sunday Telegraph*

Morbidly funny, unusual, but no basis for 'art'.

I tried to recall, first, the names of those in school with me in Adelaide, and then their appearance.

Wayne Thomas
Leslie Roach – mother died
Roger . . . (?) – whose father had a kangaroo farm
Alan McCarthy
Donald Vivien – exceptionally neat front yard
'Fatty' Roberts – the wicket-keeper
Robert . . . (?) – rolling eyes
Andrew Cheel – thick lips
Brian Norseworthy – became an RAAF pilot, and ejected into the sea
Kay Daniels – slow movements
Ian Milne – lived close to school

Ian Roberts – his dog bit me
Beverly Crabbe – large moist eyes, seemed very grown-up
Brian Coles – his brother took a job interstate

M.: 'You deserve everything that goes wrong in your life. I hope you have a lot of trouble, then you can see what you've done to me.'

Furthermore, 'You think you're so smart, reading all that philosophy you keep reading now. You think you know everything. And reading out from that book *Hinduism*, saying how good it is. Phoney! You don't believe anything beautiful, you're so harsh.'

I can remain the same. Easily.

Story. 'Raga'. Like Indian music his character can only expand in a narrow range. Final exuberance (?) is constantly held back. It is shown with several movements: him attempting change, a form of stretching, but always returning to the original self, his 'character'.

The movements within a person's character from which it cannot escape.

This urge for classification. Everywhere.

Incredibly, when descending the steps to the basement room at night I sometimes feel afraid of the dark.

'His mother's name was "Garlic".'

G. Steiner writing about science and art: at least he is not afraid to appear conservative. Recent investigations by neurologists suggest that the general preference for Rembrandt or Cézanne over abstract expressionism may not be a matter of convention. They suggest that primary visual processes are generated – matching a template of some inner harmony, in turn matching some 'classical-realistic' representation of the world.

'Atonality in modern music too, it now seems, violates certain innate expectations and equilibria of response in the nervous system.'

*The Restless Sleeper* – Magritte (Tate)

'Why on earth . . . ?' Consider the words 'on earth'.

Two dwarfs in baggy suits waddling across Fulham Road, one holding a hand up against the traffic.

On cold days my thoughts arrive faster and clearer, not blurred at the edges, as if the air no longer consists of a swirling slow-moving thickness. The cold makes me feel thin and more alert, almost pleased with myself. (Though this is felt more out on the street, not at my desk.)

I make a point of going out without a coat, or just with a raincoat. No gloves.

So cold my jaw ached.

The feeling that when it gets dark early (5 o'clock) and the lights come on, I can 'achieve' more.

Peeling a litchi with my fingers: I imagined the slippery inside of a woman.

Long clouds tinted at sunset: skeins of wool drying.

Obituary in *The Times*:

Douglas William Gumbley, CBE, ISO, who died on February 5 at the age of 92, was the inventor and designer of the first airmail letter card, while employed by the Iraq Government as their Inspector General of Posts and Telegraphs.

Normal letters, carried overland, being of

varying weight and dimensions, seemed likely to be much too expensive in those days for mass use by newly developing air services in the Middle-East. Gumbley realised the need for a lightweight form of specific size and weight. For this purpose he designed and had printed an airmail letter card which was issued by Iraq on July 15, 193–

Because I have lived in other countries and have experienced extremes (which is why I lived in other countries), I find I am using the word 'I' too much; a sign of inexperience.

Though how to penetrate the English? And why is it necessary?

This frowning may be nothing more than poor eyesight.

A dead creeper hanging over the wall like dry red hair.

Thick neck, but the soft eyes of a rabbit.

Born at a railway junction.

In India during the Indo-Pakistan war, the Cuban missile crisis, the death of Kennedy there was a run on Sunlight soap; it became a commodity, a 'hedge'. When I told this to P.B., he replied that in England during world crises sales of fishing-rods rise.

I laughed so loudly and long I almost offended him.


Even the tramps and beggars who sleep on benches and under bridges here wear a necktie. Usually maroon, dirty and loose. Strange irritation at vestiges of formality. When they ask for money I feel like not giving any.


Street in Ealing of normal red-brick houses, tiny front gardens. Suddenly a cleared block where a portable 'box house' had been removed. Only a concrete floor remained, and three armchairs flung about, their stuffing and springs exploded – mystical eruption from the suburban life.


Story. 'The Swimmer'. Man swims out alone, far out, from his family and friends seated on the beach. He visualises himself being seen by them facing him. He thinks about them, and what they must be saying etc. Shift to them and back to him. How to end?

I glanced inside the pram because the woman was too old. It was filled with dead objects – tins and vegetables sliced off at the stems.

Valetudinarium. A strain just to pronounce the wonderful word. One day I'll use it.

The English railway station (Charing Cross) is brain-shaped with the light of the outside world at one end, representing both the enclosed nature of the mind, and its wide-openness. It reverberates still with the restless energy and curiosity of the Victorians. The light angling down as in a bombed-out cathedral outlines the general mass of engineering heaviness, which is at odds with the crowd of men in three-piece suits, and women tugging at children, although in rushing away from it they do produce an industrial hum and echo.

Now, West Indian porters horsing around on Platform 9 watched by smiling but less active, skinny English porters.

From the train: rear windows of houses, plastic bottles of kitchen products lined up by consumers in a continuous line. On the top floor, many a window blocked by a bedroom mirror. (Blocking the view of the railway line, that's all.)

A mechanical landscape of cars piled up like children's toys. In the foreground, one without wheels was burning: flames wobbled out from its empty interior and licked outside the window and doors.

Curved motionless ponds with figures sitting, fishing for tiny fish. Boats lined up, all pointing one way up the canal.

The deep brown-grey of barley: beauty not only of colour but of *growth*. A large red harvester progressively eating up a field, as if all that effort was wasted.

Forests and crops, of course, contain many shadows and shades.

Manchester. Plaque in the foyer marked the spot where Henry Rolls first met Royce; or was it the other way around?

The deliberate spaciousness of hotel foyers. (A kind of vulgar lavishness.)

Never fails to put me at ease.

Morning toast and these English towns: unfortunately related.

Grey skies and wet streets half deserted.

At one end, black smoke in a tremendous horizontal rolling motion from several tall chimneys shadowed the town, the skyline jagged from the line of factory roofs in silhouette. In several directions rows of slate roofs in the drizzle appeared for a moment as wet streets. And rows of domestic chimneys like so many narrow-shouldered Englishmen standing about in coats in the rain.

In the paint factory the Technical Director sat at the end of the table: his curled fingers resting on the edge matched the curling wave of his hair. To sound more logical or to make an impression on the glut of words – at office and national level – he prefixed his argument with numbers, 'Firstly . . . Secondly . . . Thirdly' and reaching 'Fifthly . . .' turned to the letters of the alphabet, underlining each point by tapping his index fingers, 'A) . . . B) . . . C) . . .'

His young red-faced assistant in brown suit wore D.H. Lawrence's moustache.

He spoke very softly but surely on the factory floor.

A man in a thick yellow shirt who had spent all his life designing wallpapers took me aside to tell me his best designs never got through. Muttered his frustrations. I glanced at his head and he ran

24

his hand across the bald patch, 'As you can see, I've been in this game for 23 years.'

The company was engaged in a correspondence with a woman who kept finding dirty words in their printed wallpapers, especially the wood-grained series. The designer's revenge?

A puddle in the street (Manchester). It reminded me of the monsoon (Bombay).

Difference between departures at airports and ocean piers. One is a vanishing act, metallic and enclosed, the way a camera disposes of someone; the other is a formidable slow-motion rehearsal of the memory for someone fading (the liner slowly snapping streamers as it opens the gap from the wharf, the face being concentrated upon becomes out of focus, then indistinguish-able from the general mass). Hence the rather sudden tears and clutching at an airport depar-ture lounge (or relief when someone returns) and the more solemn, longer-lasting sorrow experienced among the seagulls on the pier. I am unable not to watch, and always greatly moved to see, the need people have of one another.

On railway platforms the goodbye-process is more matter-of-fact.

She'd built a living room of hair. She said many people were afraid of hair. They recoiled. In a bus or in the tube she was a normal girl, but they'd notice she had loose hair on her hands – they'd stare.

Hair is hard to get off etc.

This greyness (skin). At the time I could be acquiring tone (thoughts).

'If a book reveals to us something of which we were conscious, it feeds us with energy; if it reveals to us nothing but the fact the author knew something we knew, it draws energy from us.'                    – Pound

He gave his address as 'Artillery Mansions'. Brief envy.

Today in Berkeley Square (CLIVE OF INDIA LIVED HERE) I saw a man in pin-stripes and wearing yellow kid gloves. He had silver, precise hair and walked with a cane, giving no impression of seeing me or anybody else. So outstanding was his leanness I had the surrealist's impulse to follow him, a complete stranger, to see 'how he lived'. I even felt he would be unusually interesting to talk to. This was a Wilfred Thesiger figure who had served in some difficult colonial post – India? Ethiopia? – where he would have dispensed shrewd, experienced advice. A figure only to be seen in Britain. So exact was this impression I had almost to restrain myself from going up and asking ('Excuse me, but . . . What have you done all your life?').

Instead, I bought a ham roll and, although preoccupied, ate it hungrily.

A person's pride at *the thought of* being at the centre of a tragedy – Magritte on his mother's suicide. Yes, but this is a common feeling.

Things ('simples') are described or held by words – Wittgenstein.

Or words to that effect.

And what I know of his life in bare rooms gives each of his proposals added rigour.

Crossing the road on the way to the registry office, P. was so vague he was scraped by a bus. Waiting in the corridor: brown lino and an inordinate number of cleaning women. One down the end squatted on the floor arranging flowers. P. and S. stood up too suddenly when called. For all her hardness S. actually believed in marriage.

The ceremony at the long table, which was used for other business after hours. On the marriage certificate it said, 'Previous marriage: dissolved'. P. said, 'With nitric acid?' The sign in the parking lot, 'Look before you cross'. I said, 'For Catholic weddings?' I became only too aware of the male impulse to crack jokes, while S. held a distant smile.

If I scribble notes in the street I act as if I am ashamed.

These words:
   selenotropic
   moral ataraxy
   limn
   penetralia
   umbrageous
   gallinaceous
   mandibles (Beckett)

I am aware of the gradual and pleasant addiction to newspapers. *The Times*, *Guardian*, mostly *The Times*.

Obituary:

'R.G. writes: I first met Sir Robin Darwin – a slim figure with a menacing moustache under a broad-brimmed sombrero – when he joined the Home Office Camouflage Directorate at Leamington Spa at the outbreak of World War II. He was already a magnetic personality. He brought with him – to this exiled community of artists working as camouflage officers – a tremendous sense of style . . .' Etc.

Facts and attendant eagerness; and women patiently, sometimes fondly, smile even when bored.

Title: '*The Missionary Position*'.

'Reputed to have the most beautiful back in Hollywood' – postcard of a starlet, rear view.

While consulting the Oxford Dictionary, the pages escaped my fingers and flipped, suggesting that definitions are resisted.

As for the encyclopedia, it is always a wonder that the knowledge of the world can be contained between two cardboard covers, or rather, that the attempt has been made.

Here where the water runs out of the bath anti-clockwise . . .

Some days the stagnancy of the British and everything they've left standing resembles one of those chipped enamel tubs raised from the ground by iron paws. And the water is luke-warm and dirty, grey, with more than a few pubic hairs stuck to the enamel sides, gurgling when it runs out like a tired old man clearing his throat.

Perhaps this irritation at British complacency is only disquiet at my own nothingness here – instead of thinking of people normally (i.e. individually).

There is indifference towards me. From all sides. It can be an advantage.


Without warning the face of my father appears (as if death had removed the rest of his body and clothing). His glasses and tired eyes: unsmiling melancholy.


The doctor's wife, of small features. She'll assert herself later – much more. She wished she had met the man who had their apartment before. 'He would have been interesting. He was an interior decorator.'

The smell of the plumbers. Unlike anything else above the earth.

Shaving. Why change – reduce – what is given? Also, touching my face with my fingertips is sometimes unpleasant.

Otherwise, England is a committee.

Tossing his head, he laughed like a horse and kept on slapping his thigh to keep galloping.

The dog running with a specific errand.

The mechanic – angelic.

Sometimes I daydream of rescuing a child. In front of the mother.

In *The Times* today:
Mr David Hudson, aged 51 of Hornsey, left a suicide note in his artificial leg before setting fire to himself with paraffin. His body was found on a railway line.

1. Why his leg? It too could have burned.
2. He could have placed the note nearby.
3. Why on the railway line? For clarity? To avoid damaging other people's property? The precision of his politeness.

This nausea which now lasts all morning is worse some days than others. I am ill-tempered, sometimes dizzy, and without energy. It turns my thoughts back onto myself obsessively; and when I do look 'outside' I dwell on unpleasant, 'wrong' things. Such is the discomfort, I begin to imagine the worst and almost prefer a more tragic, slow-wasting disease – cancer, of course – instead of amoebic dysentery.

Large wart on the side of her nose like a black diamond.

Learn! Why not?

Sunset: red as the glowing tail of a jet engine. Partly because of the roar of the surrounding traffic.

Pressing my thumbs on my closed eyes I sometimes see a pattern of blurred grey squares and receding lines on a caramel wash, a strange harmony of perspective and space *I have never seen anywhere else*. If I were a painter – and even though I am not – it would be worthwhile, important even, to re-create that. But how to get the exact colours etc.? As I try to study it, gradually it begins to alter, then suddenly, goes.

M.'s goodness: so much, including words, seems to slide off her features. But then she might smile or recall something in a vague distant way.

Jeremy B.'s story about losing a Churchill tank in Germany, after the war. During manoeuvres he led a squadron into a marsh and his tank became stuck. It began to settle, then to sink. The crew scrambled out. They watched as it disappeared, 'except for its aerial'. Reporting back, he handed the officer the 'pink chit' the size of a bus ticket representing a missing tank weighing 50 tons and 'worth at least 1 million pounds'.

I noticed myself grinning: looking over his glasses, he made a point of remaining expressionless.

'I formerly admired Humboldt, I now almost adore him; he alone gives any notion of the feelings which are raised in the mind on entering the tropics.'                                              – Darwin

In England, in a basement room in London, it has the instant force of familiar evocation.

But then, as always, the sight of 'Charles Darwin' sends me back to my father. To think that an Everyman's edition of *Origin of the Species* was among the few books he had while working on a cattle station 'Arrabury', in the 1930s.

Unfortunately, everything I know about him suggests that it was fuel to his scepticism.


Artificial landscape. An artificial landscape. A terrain manufactured (by the writer) with objects and ideas passing – unfinished.


Why this illness? The feeling of being 'chosen'.


Story. Solitary pedestrian who observes solitary dweller in basement (eating with hands) and vice versa.

Reduce anything approaching 'reportage'.

Story. 'Mistaken Identity'. 'Without revealing his name, or his appearance, a series of accidents happened to this person. Without further ado here are the details.'

(List of accidents in paragraphs. Likeable and yet insignificant etc. Tone of mock formality.)


'Why are you doing this to me?'

It only made me think, What does that mean?


To the left, a man was doing up his shoelace; to the right, a man was on a ladder trimming a tree; in the centre a policeman was waving traffic forward (ridiculous iridescent sleeves); another man was stepping out of a small car with difficulty; behind me a mother was screaming at her child; above a plane was flying in a sloping straight line, filled with passengers!


Leaving the other man, he began walking backwards, and talking more loudly. Not necessarily in a hurry.


When she spoke, her lips drew back and her teeth came forward like blunt weapons.

I say 'sometimes' unnecessarily. Of course, things don't happen all the time.

M.'s aunt from Queensland: long face, wrinkled vertically (unusual). Broad sensible dress. Firm disgust of foreignness; but loud about Australia. Cost of hotels, cost of jewellery. She stole headphones from one plane for the film in the next – but wrong plug.

Reading Australian newspapers. Depressing: even the rough quality of the newsprint.

'You're looking at my nose. What's wrong?'

I enjoy shaking hands and even bowing slightly. It is tribal.

He, the architect-sewerage expert, told what they found in the sewerage pipes beneath the city: planks, tins, clothing, foetuses, lampshades, arms, legs, heads, letters, money. 'As soon as something out of the ordinary appears, the word gets around.'

A story (a paragraph) on each. The accumulative effect would suggest complexity,

movement, life, faults, sudden actions, the right-
ness of a certain direction; the city as character.


Picasso's *Weeping Woman* (Tate): an accusation
against the disintegrating face. And vice versa.
So the viewer keeps going backwards and
forwards.

The silence and serenity offered by Rothko
and Nicholson only a few paces away is not all
that reassuring.


Often I feel foolish ogling art. Especially after
stepping forward and then respectfully back
after reading a title. (The way people nearby
clear their throats as in a church gets on my
nerves.)


The beautiful woman on the street looked ugly
when she suddenly laughed.


At the publisher's warehouse the man in apron
wrapped the four books with practised system
of flicking the brown paper, somersaulting the
square pile and cutting the cord and tying: all
angles, mechanical straight lines. And the noise
made was like a man smacking his lips after a
good meal. Brown radio playing on shelf.

Smashing a lavatory seat. Somehow a lavatory is already endowed with violence.

Sunday. During a walk I noticed three old books on the step of an abandoned house. As if words were no longer being used inside.

'You devils. I could have clocked you that day.'
— Mother

The wild-eyed science presenter on television, whose specialty was the solar system, introduced a man standing in his back garden who'd made a very interesting reflector-telescope out of seven rubbish bins. He was on the verge of showing the planet (through the rubbish bins) when a cloud unfortunately passed across. 'Not to worry! We'll see it some other time.'

She slept near the pipes because it was warm.

Anxious, too anxious to have an opinion.

There is always a general untidiness about London. Now the garbage strike in its fifth week, producing enormous piles of rubbish in the streets, only confirms the idea that London would smell like any large Third World city, Calcutta, say, if it were in the tropics.

The difference (psychological, pathological) between men who choose to be
a) policemen
b) prison warders
c) museum attendants
d) traffic wardens

Beer-coloured shoes.

A.R.'s tiny dark-haired girlfriend kept a cage of hamsters on her bedside table, and as he lay with her, the little animals played on a squeaking treadmill, throwing him, he said, out of rhythm. To stop them, he felt around, found one of his socks and stuffed it in the wheel.

She lived in a cupboard, he said.

Meteorism (Hitler).

'We don't give jobs to colonials. You'll understand.'

Lying awake and considering the whole strange situation of people sleeping in cities.

'Be regular and ordinary in your life, like a bourgeois, so that you can be violent and original in your books.'
— Flaubert to a young writer (premature advice)

Garbage. Blue and black plastic bags; some burst open. Many cardboard boxes. Fish escaping from rolled-up newspapers. Dead fruit outside shops, spilling into gutters (slippery underfoot). The particular sweet smell of wet garbage.

It has transformed the city: key locations appear sandbagged, as if under siege, and streets converted into sunken alleyways by the walls of stacked rubbish. In Berkeley Square a man throwing a large bag high up onto the pile began to hurl it; but it disintegrated in his hands. His figure froze. This had never happened to him before.

And I felt satisfied at my rigour at dismantling the manuscript and tossing it onto the rubbish on the footpath outside the window, not expecting the dustmen's strike to last long. Every day I see the loose pages fluttering on top. Yesterday I noticed a woman in an overcoat and trousers standing on one of my pages; remaining near her for a second, tried a sidelong glance to see if it was a good page.

Messages tattooed on the heads of Roman slaves: sent on their way with grown hair they passed through enemy lines.

Extreme sense of duplication in everyday life. But what to do about it?

Whenever she came to the house it began raining.

Pale bankteller filled in the form so firmly with the bank's pen a spot of red spread from his fingertip – the growth of the British Empire.

The strange pleasure of rising very early, before the world gradually becomes normal again.

Sparrows shot up into the air like handfuls of dirt.

Dictionaries. Many had been published before Australia had been discovered.

Pavement.

Emerson's '*Self Reliance*': line by line, blow by blow.
I remained seated and immediately read through it again.

Socks stuffed in the ceiling of a poor man's room blocking the draughts. A ceiling of socks.

When I think of 'Australia' I first see its shape. It is quickly followed by scenes of slow-moving dryness, muted colours, and some of the great white trees. Of people in general, it is often the young, flushed mothers in sleeveless cotton dresses yanking or carrying children on the hot city asphalt.
Homesickness: habits of a landscape acquired over time.

Traces of ginger hair, not a trace of humour – the Features Editor of the Sunday paper. He never reads a novel or goes to a play. 'It's not as it is,' he said with certainty.

Pale gums lining creekbeds like women with their skirts raised.

*Jesus in India* by Hazrat Ahmed. He did not die on the cross but recovered sufficiently to go in search of the lost tribes of Israel, and gathered them together somewhere in Kashmir. According to Ahmed, His tomb was discovered in Srinagar where ancient records state it is that of the great prophet – 'Yus Assif, or the Prince of Peace, who came from Palestine.' Within such a wandering subject anything is possible.

She came back with her hair 'permed' or whatever; and I pitied her.

The door was open, things scattered all over the floor and the bed. The washbasin in the bathroom was shattered, on the floor. Three policemen crowding in were loud in their cheerful Englishness.

'What? They didn't take anything? It's one

of our kinky ones. Check your underwear. What about your underwear?'

'Mine? Why would they –'

For fingerprints he picked up the passport in the plastic envelope, and breathed on it from his red mouth.

'It's all right. We didn't have pickles for lunch.'

Etc.

The policemen told about one thief 'on our books' who leaves behind a shirt taken from a previous robbery. Several days later the victims would come across it, hidden somewhere. 'To lose your shirt . . .'

Dove-grey eyes.

The man who photographed the thought of someone.

He travelled on the train to the Midlands for the interview at Dunlop.

'The job's at the end of the production line. Throwing tyres onto a truck. All right?'

'Yes.'

'Well, what experience do you have?'

In Bond Street a young man was in the window adjusting the dress of a model. He stood alongside it, facing his boss on the footpath. The boss would touch his own elbow or knee, but the squinting window-dresser in his reversed position would adjust the wrong elbow or knee, until the man began pulling exasperated faces and moved his mouth as if shouting, though nothing could be heard through the glass.

According to van Gogh, absolute black does not exist in nature. Cézanne has written something similar.

The doctor's wife. Short, fair hair, neat. The earrings. 'He was so interesting . . .', she always says after meeting someone. On the back of her husband's watch she had engraved the dates of her birthday and their wedding anniversary. 'They've got such small brains,' she explained.

Faint nausea. But it is enough for me to think my future plans are already a failure.

A. The loudest woman in the world.

'In hot countries, nature links one to external objects and one's feelings flow gently to the outside.'                    – de Stael

Woman who survived her three sons. On their headstone she had had engraved: ONE WOMB, ONE TOMB.

Story. A place (country, a distance) where movement has deliberately been made difficult – as pre-Perry Japan – where rivers have no bridges, there are unnecessary slopes, narrow paths, dead ends, instructions. Someone's life in material form.

Clergyman who adjusts wedding speech to the profession of grooms. Actors, for example: 'checking your parts, the right role for each other, don't be late, etc.'
    The front row full of broken marriages.

Ears, Diseases of.

His tremendous ordinariness.

H.R. Grey-faced Jew, grey hair pushed back, always in need of a trim (long loose hairs). And wide moustache, though not wider than his mouth, which gives the mouth that extra horizontality. Strangely old-fashioned in speech, manner and appearance – as though he had lived a long time. A clerk in Somerset House. Lives alone in bare rooms in Soho. Old cream walls, lino floors. He reads only old work, mainly the Greeks. Never opens a newspaper.

After offering duty-free apricot brandy he served spaghetti from a tin, and spoke loudly.

He can no longer let friends stay in his flat, and in telling me began enjoying himself. A certain rhetorical rhythm:

'I'm tired now. I don't feel like telling them where the stove turns on, and over-filling the bath makes the water come through the woman's ceiling below me, and I've got to tell them not to put the radiator too close to the chairs as it'll burn the varnish. They perhaps think I'm barbaric turning them away from my door. But I didn't know him in particular anyway, I didn't know what he was like.'


The word 'citizen' implied conspiracy.


His greatest gift was to remain neutral, and with ease he passed through to the top.

Newspaper advertisement, Ecuador:

'ESTEEMED MISTER THIEF.

I beg you to consider the series of problems which have resulted from those personal documents (driving licence, voting card etc.) and the need I have of the four key-rings with nearly fifty keys which you without any bad intention borrowed from my motor car on Wednesday 23rd in the afternoon.

The tape recorder I offer to you as a commission in recognition of the return of the objects I mentioned.

I hope you will keep the briefcase too.

I know you have a good heart.'

The laborious courtesy and the man's mysterious (50 keys?) possessions fit my fascination and preconceptions of Latin America, acquired through literature. The Chilean with the stiff grey crewcut who showed me this kept laughing at it: a kind of homesickness.

Rabies victim. He turns into the animal by recalling key memories, and then having no memories. No memory (or intellect) but only instinct. So he dies unafraid of death (like the animal inside him). He has returned to the original non-pleasurable form. A violent devolution. Story.

In the country – England – a tree on a farm broke branches on two occasions and on the same days a member of the family died. It was decided the tree had given a 'sign'. So they scaffolded it, preventing more branches from falling, and the tree's natural function was altered.

'At the Tropical Diseases Hospital I . . .'

13.12.70. St Pancras. Old fences of iron, hard angles, girders, railway bridges, rows of parked trucks (fogged windscreens), grey gas-storage tanks, cars parked beneath overhead-railway lines; and men trudge about in rubber boots and short dark coats.

Landscape near hospital.

'The penalty of an Eastern education . . .' The sardonic sympathy of the examining doctor. But while he spoke his eyes wandered around the rest of the ward.

The long hours put in by doctors and nurses are counterbalanced by the enormous amount of healthy walking.

Outside, fog filled the spaces between the black trees. A perpetual shunting from the railway yards: the sudden rising and falling racket of the diesels, like DC3s taxi-ing and throttling back on tarmacs, followed by the rattle of metal and a creaking which is multiplied. Above the row of trains: white seagulls against the grey. These trains are part of the daily equation of shifting other citizens to offices, shops, factories (moving of freight from one place to another, too), while in the ward we read or lie, immobile. The whole day is open. Like the tropics the atmosphere is slow, waiting. To make us feel more at home the ward is overheated.

At the meal table or around the tea urn at 10 o'clock patients discover people and old hotels other patients knew – Africa, mainly.

Boat shaped shoes, Kohlapuri *chappals*, embroidered slippers, dragons on silk dressing gowns, plain haircuts, and the curious way people in the tropics stand with a cup and saucer.

A sub-world of types I slightly belong to.

Merchant sailor with fungus on his kidneys, now affecting his heart. Young, pitted face, dreams of girls – practised familiarity with nurses, of one accustomed to hospitals.

Metering technician who drank water on an African train 28 years ago. Since then he has vomited once a week and has diarrhoea. Again, that overfamiliar breeziness with nurses. Has a working-man's sense of fair play (or more, the declaration of it): 'A bloke must take his turn. He'd better watch out with me if he doesn't.' Suddenly he lets out a loud yawn.

Old round woman in soft brown. She was bitten by a rabid cat.

Young nun, dressed in white. From Nigeria. Pale, silent. But she has an unexpected, raucous laugh and spoke rather jauntily of her uncomfortable experiences.

Pakistan woman, sharp, grey, beautiful face. Slouched over her meal from the habit of eating with her hands.

Chinless Englishman from Crown Agents who always wore a tie and oriental slippers. Been everywhere. Had that British eagerness when talking history.

Two extremely black men from Uganda. The one in the bed next to me had 'aching joints'. The other one, Tom, had an African disease – worms laid eggs under the skin, travel to the eyes. He was allergic to all their cures. Noticing that the days in London are colder than the nights he said, 'Here the moon is hotter than the sun.'

Little East African boy who played in the corridor with plastic snake.

Stout Englishman. With extremely 'energetic' teeth.

Plain woman from Yorkshire who was embarrassed to say at the table (when everyone was revealing their ailments) that she had a tapeworm. 'It must be a whopper if you've got to come into hospital,' said the metering technician. She lived with her husband near Lucknow. Later she told me she saw a tiger one night in the headlights of an open jeep.

Gangly West Indian boy who trips and punches out of a kind of loneliness. 'What d'you want to be when you grow up?' After everybody tried guessing (around the table) he confessed: a gymnast, like those in the Commonwealth Games. He gazed at the wall; certainly serious. Age: 13.

Skinny thin-lipped Goan. Like a senile lawyer, always presenting both sides. 'On the one hand . . .' And, 'Then of course . . .' And his unembarrassed use of the absolute cliché. He is always wanting to talk (stands at the foot of my bed, both hands in his dressing gown). Enlarges on his hypochondria. A name-dropper to this extent: 'I wrote a memorandum to Indira on that. I know her very well . . .' Or, 'My friends in the Cabinet . . .'

53-year-old stumpy Scot. Who was led to the bed opposite by his wife – came into the room wearing a glossy brown fur coat. She talks on, he waits, then continues, not taking any notice of her. Leaving, she reeled off half a dozen Christian names she said she'd phone. Nurse: 'Have you opened your bowels today?' He: 'Hummmmph. They haven't been shut.' Struggling out of bed he groans, 'Oh Jesus Christ.' After medication, he said to me, 'I was here seven days ago. Now I'm back.' He offered me home-made biscuits. He's an attendant at the Victoria & Albert. 'Everybody calls me "Jock".'

The farmhand: in the corner, very shy. He had a rare skin disease from ('they say') handling imported sheep. Not only had he never been to the tropics, he had visited London only three times, although he lived and worked all his life on the same farm only 30 miles away. 'You can see the glow on some nights.' To be so close to such a huge thing and have no desire . . . He was almost 70. Told he could leave, he was seated on the edge of the bed dressed, packed and shaved by 6 a.m., more like a plump priest summoned to the bed of a dying man. His son had to collect him. The son arrived around 10.

Left wearing a cloth cap, happy.


Night. The Ugandan vomited in the washbasin, while 'Jock' talked in his sleep.


The clergyman came in the afternoon. Soft, plump, dull public-school voice. During the silence, he too looked outside: 'Mmmmm. Another train . . .'


The eminent Professor of Tropical Medicine came in with attentive acolytes trailing like his flapping coat-tails. He glanced at the novel beside my bed and almost smiled: *The Vivisector*.

The professor said to the Crown Agents man in a Madras cotton bush-shirt: 'I want everybody in pyjamas.'

Patients/patience. But the etymologists will say the first originates somewhere else.

Always the distant footsteps in the hospital, even at night.

M.'s visit: I felt lazy, defenceless as she stood at the end of the bed in her outdoor clothes. Faint awkwardness.

The woman bitten by the rabid cat. Tomorrow is the crucial 14th day. The pale seaman is going around taking bets on whether rabies (and certain death) has become established. Eating at the table she appeared unconcerned.

Young, very mannish woman who briskly disinfects the headphones every week on contract has no intention of talking.

The advance hum of the floor-polisher is soothing. While I'm lying in bed.

The irregular bumping sound means it is hitting the skirting boards. For some reason this pleases me.

'Jock' said to the nervous Goan about to have a special investigatory rod stuck up his arse: 'You'd have to pay for it at the West End.'

The larger of the two Ugandans is a school-teacher. Slow, gentle man with the peculiar figure of an African in clothes: head leans forward, stomach hangs out and checked by a low belt, and enormous plain black shoes (in Africa they'd be dusty). He speaks with simple dignity. He says 'man' and 'woman' in their natural original sense. He spent hours describing the stages of his marriage. He calls the nurses 'madam'. 'Excuse me, madam.' He said Uganda was God's country. He meant the perfect weather and the animals, and 'if you want a house everybody else helps you build it'. On the way to X-rays he asked if they take five years off a man's life. 'Is it true? Someone has told me.' He asked me to stand beside him; and during it he didn't take his eyes off me.

Boy selling the newspapers in the ward: strange coming in from the outside in street clothes, displaying a cold face.

A Pole arrived with terrible scars across his face. He got those, he said, when he was six in Siberia, wrapped in fur, dragging wood. Wolves attacked, thinking he was a dog. In the tropics he . . .

Something in his hasty manner made me begin to doubt his words.

Everybody concentrated on the end bed. The curtains were suddenly pulled back like the beginning of a play: a stranger, horizontal, with an open mouth.

'What do you want to know the time for? Nobody's going anywhere.'

When he spoke his body seemed to shiver from the cold.

If I wasn't a 'writer', I'd somehow move about inside a hospital.

Only the doctors are impersonal here.

A novel as a giant hospital.

'I'm told that bugger down the end's got worms.'

The expressionless Nigerian told me his friends,
all men, had the Christian names of English
flowers ('Daffodil', 'Rose', etc.) and surnames
'Sea never dries', 'No king is god', 'Chief big
dick', etc.

From Mali and he said he was writing a novel in
his own language, not French. His visitors were
thin and urgent young Englishmen.

His act (in clubs to the north) consisted of
revolving a bowl of goldfish on the end of a
string, looping the loop, twirling and forming
patterns. After complaints from the RSPCA he
could continue only if he used carrots. 'So there
was no point after that. Know what I mean?'

'Jock' had fought behind the lines in Burma.
After the war – six years in Burma and India –

he couldn't settle down. England was boring. London depressing. He had a different woman every night. With three years' back-pay he bought a cabin-cruiser. He set himself up on a river, but it was a terrible winter and he became frozen in. Trapped, he got malaria; the doctors couldn't get to him. 'There I was shivering with my own thoughts.' Looking back on all this, he laughed at himself. He couldn't settle down. 'I'd be creeping through the jungle with my machine gun. I didn't want someone telling me what to do.' He punched foremen. He had 120 different jobs before the V&A, where he was the union representative.

He married when he was 35. 'Watch it, here she comes now.'


'Yairs' – P. White. Confidence on the author's part.


He too kept saying, 'Know what I mean?'


So-and-so already licking his top lip although he's barely in his thirties.


A certain briskness on the part of the nurses seems necessary. The Scottish sister.

'I'm the matron, but I'm not so bad.'

9.9.70. Anniversary of the Blitz. As the others slept, I lay in the dark listening with head-phones to reminiscences of events I would never experience. (This attraction to extremes, as if it might reveal something basic.)

Burning frocks in shops. Burning dummies. Burning stockings floated down from the sky.

Sanitation so bad in the tube shelters people even left them.

The looter who was tripped overloaded with glass eyes. They stared at him.

Old people crack first. Weary wardens would go back to a site early in the morning with a girl to look for her doll.

Stone-deaf man the only one who remained at nude show during heavy raid. Windmill Theatre.

A girder became red hot and sagged.

Entire front of house fell away and revealed man in bathroom.

People insisted on traditional funerals with procession, biers etc.

Wild rumours of special weapons. There was a 'spring bomb that expands and decapitates'. A man heard one land and ran – something whooshed and clattered past him. He fell to the ground and waited. 'When I lifted my head I discovered it was a bleedin' rubbish bin.'

Outside the hospital I observed everything with special alertness. And the shop windows, the signs on buildings, the figures casually going about their business seemed to be a product of *cold air.*

I wanted to see more of this. But in a few minutes I had joined them – with a certain weakness of the limbs.

Windswept hair, bad teeth. He also had short fingernails.

Ponderous, exact, unhappy man (moist, pursed lips) absorbed in model trains. His wife: 'If I started playing with dolls at my age, they'd lock me away.'

Why do they wear rings? (Women.)

A story consisting entirely of footnotes. Provisional.

The only exercise he took was shaving.

Sometimes I over-enthuse like an amateur.

'Use *delay* instead of "picture" or "painting".'
— Duchamp

Story. Sahara, or Afghan in Australia, camel driver. His birth is not recorded, he knows his age by the number of caravan journeys, and his death is not recorded. In his 'time' he lives in simple seasons — heat, cold, animals, fire. He exists like sand. Camel's famous haughty expression.

Maya Indians of Guatemala: suicides were believed to go straight to heaven, as a result of which people took their lives on small pretexts. (Their mathematics, invention of zero.) Bishop Landa described — with nervous respect — a time-measuring device called a Katum-wheel, which made it easy for a man to recall events that had happened 300 years before.

Cloud studies (Constable). I respect that.

Certainly many more muscles are involved in smiling than frowning. Check.

Too often I feel: lack of goodness.

Paris. Christmas 1970. Snow floating down as if pillows were being shaken. Workmen with cold blue hands. Buildings with their vaulted roofs like the brown helmets of deep-sea divers; and sculptured figures silhouetted on top like men preparing for suicide. One reason why Paris surrendered during the War: it is too beautiful – elegant, civilised – to be destroyed. Eden reportedly said to Petain, 'There are more things than buildings and monuments, you know.' But Petain didn't appear to hear.

The way Paris people sit at café tables and study the pedestrians passing. A transparency between the two, which continues in winter through the temporary glass walls.

Woman (in shop): 'Why are we queuing?'
Man: 'Take it easy. It's Christmas.'
Woman: 'Are you talking to me?'

D.G., the American academic, led me around to show where Hemingway and Fitzgerald had lived. Little interest for me except Hemingway's first address (1926?). On the first floor above what had been a sawmill, it made his efforts appear more industrious; at the same time more ordinary, hopeful, close to failure. The building and its shadow remain basically unchanged, but 'pointing'.

S. Beach's Shakespeare & Co. Bookshop. Now a dress shop, but the building solid enough to reveal, or rather preserve 'history'.

Middle-aged man on roller skates in the foreground of the Eiffel Tower. Almost too old to be enjoying himself.

Scrawled over poster outlawing wall-writing (near Sorbonne): TO FORBID IS FORBIDDEN.

Alongside Cézanne, the Impressionists appear hesitant. The very principle of catching the passing mood and moment (of light etc.) could be working against them.

The *Red Interior* of Matisse is jammed with confidence.

Three young men were pushing a Volvo into the rue de Seine. Two cars behind them began hooting their high-pitched horns – and wouldn't stop. The men stopped pushing, went back, and began shouting at them. One grabbed the driver of a blue Citroën, his foot slipped off the clutch pedal, jumping the car forward, ramming the next car, which then crashed into the car being pushed. The abrupt movements and the sound of breaking glass accelerated their aggression. Everybody punching. The Volvo driver began crouching and showing his teeth, kicking and retreating like a rabid monkey. His friend took an umbrella from the Volvo and running forward jabbed one of the others off-balance – who seemed to lie on the ground too long. They were all fearful, outside their experience.

Still, why does my heart beat faster watching other men fight? Why do I want to watch? I put myself in the place of one of them, with little success.

For no apparent reason I remember the semi-aerial rustiness of Brisbane. It is quickly corrected by the 'cleanliness' of Adelaide.

Wife (in shop): 'It's too big.'
Man: 'It should be smaller.'
Wife: 'It's just not small enough.'
Man (nodding): 'No, it's bigger than we need.'

Strolling from one picture to another in art galleries, even commercial ones, I am assailed by literary ideas which beg to be resolved.

The Greek merchant Hippalus (1st century BC), who discovered the full use of monsoon winds to and from India, and Hipparchus (190 BC) with his *catalogue* of 850 stars.

I am slouching more. Now M. is commenting.

Throughout the duration of the film (*The River*) an uncomfortable man in the aisle opposite knelt on the floor, as if in prayer – out of the corner of my eye.

Music can always be relied upon to induce melancholia. As it progresses, it represents in a gentle, heightened sense the loss of the very thing it passes through – time.

In the motel in L.A he pulled back the curtain and found only a bare wall. So he couldn't sleep that night.

'I sought to free my inner life from any alien influence, to look with love on all around me, and allow all beings, from man downwards to the lowest comprehensible creature, to act upon me, each after his own kind. Thus arose a wonderful affinity with the several objects of nature, and a heartfelt concord and harmony with the whole, so that every change, whether of place and country, of hour or season, or of any part of the natural order, affected me profoundly.'

– Goethe

The way Edwardian women face the camera with folded fans hanging from their waists like razors.

I enquired about Malcolm F. of Adelaide and was told he had cut away half his eyebrow to help his archery, and had opened a hair-dressing salon in his dead father's garage. Only the outstanding features of a life are recalled.

The yogi called 'Time'. Having the name of Time, and moving through a landscape. And the vengeance of Drona: capturing a king who expects death but is made 'half a king' so that his captor can enjoy his friendship. Affection on equal terms.

— *Myths of the Hindus and Buddhists*

Young Englishman, his face was old on his body and round as an apple. He looked worried. At the same time he wore an expression of boredom.

'Remember her? She went off and married a Canadian.'

Cold night: steam rising from yellow neon sign.

Cold night: tramps under the bridge at Charing Cross, their feet in cardboard boxes.

Cold morning. So many pedestrians seemed to have 'physical liabilities'. Arms missing, one eye closed, teeth out, limping, etc.

Sign on factory: TIME COMPANY.

Kneeling to say his prayers at school he was tapped on his shoulder by the priest, 'Speak up, I can't hear you'. 'I'm not talking to you,' he replied, still kneeling. Now a chubby journalist.

Famous travel-writer, N. Large red head, piano teeth. He and A.R. guffawing, A.R. banging the table at some of the stories (Englishmen in club). The loudness of N.'s conversation, which went on like a train rattling over points, bridges, viaducts, accompanied by the clinking of cutlery, left me increasingly stone-faced. Why is he talking so much – with such ease? Sensing my sourness he became attentive, almost over-polite. And on the footpath as we departed he waved his furled umbrella, his tie loose from his collar, like an old man. Then I felt perplexed, slightly ashamed at my aloofness in the face of his healthy enjoyment of life, which includes claret and port.

On the title page of certain paperbacks: 'Manufactured in the United States'.

Religion: I don't know.

He had a collection of spears in his living room.

Rather prim woman who lives alone: almost 40. Visiting friends in Australia, she said the outback was like being in the middle of a women's magazine serial. Station-owners seemed to be on the verge of proposing to her. The wife of one was a 'Brisbane bitch', and she would have stayed if it wasn't for her. To make her stay he gave her rum every night for three months.

There is no such thing as 'History'; only erudition?

Has the sour look of a girl who argues with her mother.

Fortification, not imagination (Britain).

She collected memories of things, as other people collect objects. She hurries to fill the hours of her life. Naturally, she turned to photography.

Barcelona, 13.2.71. City of overhead wires and small birds in cages. Skinned rabbits in windows, their eyes intact. Men smoking the fat cigar. Much else is coffee-coloured, including leather.

70

Hotel room had keys with chains like rosary beads.

Exceptionally fleshy noses.

Freezing high rooms in the museum in the old palace filled with repetitious religious art. The attendant with the enormous, almost false, purple nose followed me to explain how much clothing he had to wear. He pointed: 'Rubber soles, false sole, two socks. Otherwise you can't live here.'

The Barcelona architect. Bachelor, 52. Crewcut going grey, small Spanish moustache, shoulders like a T-square. The penthouse filled with small beautiful objects arranged carefully. Each item of sculpture, textile and print positioned precisely, without a grain of dust, illuminated by tiny lamps. Every few minutes he went off and selected, like a librarian, a book to illustrate a point. All his books were illustrated books. Presentation lithographs from Miro, Picasso, Tapies aligned in rows as evidence. 'These are priceless now,' he waved to the carpets. Pouring whisky: 'People don't know what they're talking about when they criticise Spain. We are free here, as much as any country. I can take 5000p out of this country, which is a lot of money for a poor country. Franco is all right. But I'm not saying I'm a Franco.' Sweeping his arm around the room, 'This place is too small. I have designed my own house in Barcelona. It has a swimming pool, garden and sauna bath. I find myself getting back to the simple things of life now – water, earth and perspiration.' His brother is a Benedictine monk at the Monserrat monastery.

He took us out for pizzas. The act of generosity, the gesture, made him more expansive. He became more talkative, holding our arms. Then as evidence of his power and goodness (the pizzas) disappeared he made himself absolutely likeable by heaping praise on us – through the other person. To M.: 'You're a very lucky woman. He's quite a nice guy.' Praising one through the medium of the other, he created a doubly favourable impression. 'But then you nice people came in. Are we friends?'


Teruel. Streets dotted with blind people.


In the hotel dining room, six commercial travellers at six separate tables, and posters on the wall of small birds looking up at a small airliner.

Corners of building chipped with bullet marks. The cold.

Underestimate the size of crowds.

On a river, facing a desolate plain. The fighting around Teruel during the Civil War described as 'bitter'. It was already a bitter landscape.

Ageing men with heavy heads pitted like the walls. Because of this their faces appear to come forward more.

The Teruel school-teacher who defended the town for the Republicans. Bumpy face and bulging blackheads like the worn gouged land across the river. 'I was a democrat, not a Communist,' he repeated twice, then three times. After the war he was in jail for '39 months and 23 days (pause) less 6 hours'. Lowering his voice only slightly, he said the man he greeted in the bar was the one who had arrested him.

Because 'time' simply continues, towns and people have little option but to 'continue' also. But in an uneven, broken way.

Man ploughing field with horse stood on the plough like a water skier.

Scattered white rocks looked like sheep in the distance.

Tall thin trees stripped of leaves could have been a row of feathers.

Pink village embedded in rocks. Small green river.

Signs again that men had committed themselves. A small high window of the church was surrounded by bullet marks. Inside, it was above the precious altar. The sniper's muddy boots must have been on the altar. Albarracin.

The way buildings cluster (villages). That is, people huddle together.

Endless unhurried sound of water.

What does the Spanish shepherd with scarf wrapped around his face alone with his sheep, in barren landscape, think about? With gaps or 'slownesses' following the contours of the earth? Uncluttered by the large city distractions and the comparisons with many other people? And he would read very little, if at all. With his head down, watching the ground, the sheep appear forgotten.

The Electrified Village. Thunder – thick in the sky. The creek sped. Shutters were closed. Horses ran down the main street, a black one in front. Bells chimed from the church tower, but were amplified – a scratchy recording. Positioned below the bell the tinny loudspeaker was the same shape.

Spanish men in café (fogged-up windows). Even if women were allowed, there would be no room.

The office window looks down on side street, W1. At 3.30 every day I watch the street-cleaners returning to their depots, pushing their aluminium trolleys (with rubber wheels) which hold brooms, metal pans and rubbish. Very punctual. A long scattered line. They walk slowly. Mostly they remain apart. One or two lean Englishmen stand out; the proud ones come in last as if they don't want to be part of the group. Cold day. They wear gloves. A few don't – hands red, they grip the bar.

There is a joker, always the same, and usually ignored.

'I'm 14 years older than the Eiffel Tower' – Isadora Duncan's hyperactive brother. Story (with the Sydney Harbour Bridge).

He was transferred from the London office to Karachi with his English wife. She hated it. She ran off with an American. Rigid and powerful, but much affected, the businessman had a large sentimental portrait painted of her, and got R.A. to deliver it personally, in San Francisco. An Eastern move. She could never destroy it; nor could she display it.

Absence of music.

Writing: a form of dark vegetation (spreading).

I felt blank at what she was saying about me and at the same time – appalled. Then a kind of careless helplessness.

Briefly in the street: I have seen another man like him in another part of the world. And they know the other exists.

Stories (shapes): 1) Tear-shaped – pressure, release 2) Homage to the Square 3) Zigzag 4) The triangle 5) Flat story, hammered by events beyond the character's control, bulging the centre, into something strong.

The hood of his coupé was eaten by cows.

'And so on and so forth. You know what I mean.'

Labials. Pertaining to lips etc.

Reputations exceed a person's private opinion of himself.

Near Berkeley Square early in the mornings a tiny woman wearing a hat with fruit and veil gets down on her knees and mops the steps of an office block. 'She's always been like that. She had a son who drowned – off the Isle of Man, unless I'm mistaken.'

Geoffrey U. He was out of work for seven months and at a party met a man whose partner owed him money. Within seconds G. mentioned it, speaking rapidly and over-casually. And so he raised his chin and rolled his head like a camel trying to swallow something large. The other one subtly defended his partner. 'Was it for services rendered, or a product you sold?'

His hands trembled from regular hangovers, but he managed to land a job – in the China Department at Harrods. When the store manager came around to meet the newcomers G. bowed, and his bum knocked over a porcelain partridge.

'I maintain that cynicism borders on chastity.'
– Flaubert

To write but to avoid becoming a 'writer'. This feeling against is insistent and true.

The television arts interviewer took three times the lethal dose of barbiturates. In his note to his brother, 'I cannot bear it any longer, but I don't know what it is.'

Novelist, playwright, homosexual, he lived in a '300 year old cottage' and spent the last few years interviewing other people about their beliefs. In television's world of harsh verbal exploitation he was tender.

Like everybody else I take an interest in my own shadow. Just checking.

In the room above, a man and woman argued violently every night. Then she died. In the silence without her he became drunk – singing, knocking furniture over, and usually retching. We would hear him flush his vomit away and it rush and gurgle past in the pipes in our room.

From Langham Street looking up: his window always closed. I saw him this morning: grey face, coarse moustache, a woollen scarf tucked in around the collar of his coat, stepping out.

Personality depends on the persistence of memory.

Priest (short back and sides) had given up his job and hitchhiked around the country. With each driver he'd plant a casually-spoken religious message. He'd get off at a town, and catch another driver. Very methodical. Up and down the country.

Just as he never won anything in a lottery, he would be the first to be killed in a war.


Without straining for effects.


To think some women are married to funeral directors, or to mortuary workers, or sleep with surgeons who make inspections inside the bodies of women every day – accustomed to bodies in a dispassionate sense.


The radio-controlled model plane hit a champion racehorse.


In Yugoslavia her father would bring his girl-friends into the house after midnight and wake her up to read their fortunes. 'The creep,' she smiled. Details of their lives were told to her the day before. But she loved him. In London he wore a bright blue suit, normal for a European opera singer, and wondered why he was stared at. What else? From Yugoslavia he smuggled out paintings in the crates of scenery for an impoverished artist who lived in their house eating all their food.

Rounded brown moors (Yorkshire) stained with shadows. Fenceless in places. The smaller sky.

Near the road two middle-aged farmers helped a sheep give birth. Clear sky, bright green grass. They were talking quietly in their country accents. One was grunting. He had his arm inside the ewe, up to his elbow, pulling at the lamb. After much tugging it came out, dead.


Extreme alertness to almost all things. Which is suddenly dulled when I begin talking to someone.


*Thoughts and Details on Scarcity*


Thin old man seated in the corner of the bar. 'You know why I like dogs? Because they don't talk. Dogs don't drop bombs on each other, and talk.' The dog walked away. 'Everyone talks. Words, words instead of getting down and doing things.'

He grabbed N.'s hand for the matches. 'Here, this is what it's all about. Give me.'

He lit the match, put it in his mouth, and closed his mouth.

The Buddhist monk in South Vietnam who made a landscaped miniature 'Vietnam', complete with contours, and took a symbolic walk down its length every day.


The parking meter whirred like a rattlesnake.


Obituary:

Captain Cyril Falls, CBE, died yesterday, aged 83.

Scholar, author and soldier, he was Military Correspondent to *The Times* from 1939 until 1953 and was . . .

Falls was a delightful man of modest and unassuming character, and a charming and loyal friend. He was slightly built and always immaculately turned out. All his life he cultivated a somewhat military air which was enhanced by a brushed-up moustache. He prided himself upon having had an excellent tailor for over 40 years, and he used to say he was not conceited about anything except his clothes. Etc.


Mr Smallacombe and the canary. It was his mother-in-law's canary. (Also his RSL badge.)

His legs were so short I calculated his navel at precisely his body's centre.

He squinted, even when asleep.

A family all fighting (hitting) each other.

The bookseller in the rue Jacob, the late Pierre Lambert, who was the world's authority on Huysmans, had the perfectionist's fatal flaw: if he did not know what Huysmans had for breakfast on a certain day in December 1897 he could not embark on his life. He gave the task to someone called Baldick, 30 years of his research, free.

She worked for the railways as a shorthand typist; she took down the details of suicides for the railways reports.

Contempt of photography. Why not?

Getting into his dark coat he hunched up, contracted himself, went narrow in the face, before becoming upright, the way an umbrella is suddenly opened.

After a few vodkas, surrounded by four men, and listening to their speedy assertive asides, she suddenly burst into tears.

She went to the ladies' room then walked outside and caught a cab. The bumps of the cab threw her about; she concentrated on the man's driving. She realised she was half drunk. The cab stopped at her door.

'You did me a good turn. My girlfriend lives near here, and it's a long trip without the meter. My wife's gone to Manchester, so I can see my girlfriend . . .'

He was an old man. This made her more depressed. She looked at him and ran inside.

Her name was Sheila.


May Day, Hyde Park 1971. Now they reclined on the grass, half listening to speeches. The older men – in their late fifties and sixties – were the remnants of the British Left of the 30s with the obstinate appearance of vegetarians: glaring eyes, pipes, sandals. They would never be in the majority. The young displayed a certain pre-dictability of the new arrivals: beards, badges, babies. Their loyal women almost untidy in their informality.


*The Man Who Married My Sister*
*The Man Who Built the Pyramids* (Blake)

*Venus, Cupid, Folly and Time* (Bronzino)
*Cul-de-Sac*


M.'s hairdresser went for excitement and
married Rodriguez, the Mexican racing driver,
who was killed. Now back in London combing
women's hair.


When I wake up, I have to remember myself and
all that has gone before to continue. If not?


On the wall of the National Gallery: Arthur
Boyd's dog!


He was felled by the petal of a rose. Possible.


Borges at the ICA. Led onto the stage by R.
Lowell. With his tilt of the head and protruding
lip he looked like one of those rare fish coming
up from the deep with milky eyes. Or rather,
an incredibly precocious boy disturbed in an
immense library, looking up surprised he has
become old.

So it is possible for a good writer to wear a
suit and necktie.

In the shelter down the backyard during the blitz she shouted, 'I've left me false teeth inside.' He shoved her down. 'They're dropping bombs, not fucking sandwiches.'

Ordinary view of the artist here. Auden as a plumber etc. So no surprises.

Black houses, green valleys. Nothing moves on the green.

Beautiful town ruined by its name: Bath.

Zum, glitch, jabberwockies, basilisk (fabulous creatures).

The thin neurotic Anglo-Indian in Bombay who told me he could find his way home to his door at night by the smell of a nearby dead bandicoot. Invited me there to meet others like him.

'He should have been killed in the First World War.'

Story. Inside an office. Semi-aerial view. The partitioned rooms of each occupant and what they say. Decorations, tidiness. It's possible to climb over (hurdling).

Kpelihe masks were used to remind people of human imperfections.

Church in a lane near Langham Street. Someone has scraped on the door a cross in human shit.

The Sicilian father who tried to insure his daughter's virginity when she went off to work as an au pair in Germany was turned down by Lloyd's, because losing your virginity 'is not an accident', and she could always have done it 'to spite her father' or to help him out of a difficult 'financial corner'.

Why do they (nurses) walk outside the hospital with their arms folded?

But it is good in this vast city at 9pm to see that it is still light. 'To see' – it is more a feeling of optimism.

He needed some streak of evil, some extremity, to show itself so that she could use her gentleness and kindness. As it was, they were too matched.

There was therefore no attraction of sex.

At Covent Garden as I look away from the stage and see the shafts of light and the motionless shapes of men and women in their boxes, I am sharply reminded that the same thing occurred fifty or a hundred years before. Nothing had changed except different people were now in the same seats; the building containing them remains the same. And this audience is engrossed, oblivious!

The deaf old woman at Ealing had a young couple as boarders. She phoned her three children and told them it had rained. They made fun of her, suggesting she was mad. The old woman then asked the young couple to phone each of her children to prove that it had rained, while she stood beside them.

Brighton pier: white as a Southern paddle-steamer, half covered in barnacles.

The chemist absurdly proud of his jars.

D. relating his wife's tantrums:

'As we're sitting around, I'm minding my
own business, she gradually in full view pulls
out a hand-grenade and slowly raises her arm
and sails it over almost in slow motion at my feet,
where it settles, then suddenly goes bang. I'm
still fairly relaxed, although I feel my patience
go; I want to get back to what I was doing. But
by this time she has brought up bazookas,
mortars, bayonets, artillery, you name it.'

He always remembered the morning in 1938 he
left Bombay, sitting among his luggage. The
wharf had a loose plank, and a white post with
scratches, a coil of rope beside it. Thirty years
later he returned in his own ship. Nothing had
changed: the plank still loose, the white post
there with the scratches, the rope coiled as he
had left it. Even the Moslem with a long white
beard was squatting in the same position, he
said.

29.6.71. One year in UK.

Being layered by texture; the comparisons.
The grey is of typefaces – words.

There is always enough commonsense here to despise it.

British gentleness and reason. Complacency.

As a small girl in Ireland, she watched as a man fell from a ferry and, sinking from the pounds of tea and rice hidden about his body, drowned.

'Newsletter from H.M.' Expatriate photographer who had lived for many years near Madras with an Indian wife. He collects snakes, has them inside the house (one moving along my neck while on the sofa) and dispenses medicines to the village. His empire, the village; his special sort of deliberate breeziness. Each year he mails a newsletter telling what he has done, his travels, news of snakes, reduction of dysentery in his village. His huge wife occupies half a sentence.

Berwick Street. Two madmen shouting to each other as they searched in the rubbish for unsquashed fruit.

Depressed by his intuitions.

In Poe's story 'Loss of Breath', the man who was the originator of 'tall monuments – shot-towers – lightning rods – Lombardy poplars. His treatise upon *Shades and Shadows* has immortalized him'.

A beggar close to the ground moving from A to B.

At least the good sense and dreary stability of England, which extends into literature, provokes in me an opposing, forceful stance, which in turn is so abhorrent to the English it is rejected out of hand.

Today I am sick of my own voice and opinions.

In Czechoslovakia he buried a stamp collection in the country; whenever he wanted to leave, he would take one of his beloved stamps, walk out, and sell it in Vienna.

Hampstead Heath. Man threw a model plane for the first time with his girlfriend watching.

Crashing instantly, breaking a wing. I quickly turned away, for her sake.

Mysterious passage of air in the coal mine. Tunnels, ladders, rooms with electric light bulbs, ledgers, lavatories. Clocks, rosters and printed signs; a society in darkness. Black on black, as a Reinhardt painting.

The explosion. Bare feet. Sound of bells.

Without meaning to, the tunnels form a letter or a monogram.

Think of any black surface and I see a face emerging.

Before becoming a motor-cycle stuntman he sold 110 insurance policies in one day in a lunatic asylum.

Dream. I was on (or positioned near) a thick varnished mast. The seas a deep green. Foaming ridges. It was a brief view: suddenly in close up a long sailing ship without masts embedded in permanent grey ice. It was there like land in the middle of the ocean. I stepped on board — deserted — and into a different world. I was below deck, a pavilion without rooms. I had to stoop. Ice-encrusted wooden shelves. There were heads of men — with additional layers of flesh about the mouth and eyes. I studied these in sympathy, and the eye of one fluttered at me. Slave-like figures lay about after exhausting tasks, half encrusted in ice. Grey. And a long interior perspective. Then I was back on deck – to a kind of cobweb atmosphere. Someone was trying to 'escape' in a small Austin car. Two wheels were on the ice. I waited for it to crash through – a tragedy. But, no. I watched it drive away. It was my father's grey Austin.

Living in England I find I am using the semicolon more, as if all statements here are qualified.

Woman strolling along using a walking stick – upside down.

Mr History (1). Not only is T.D. suspicious of anything modern but turns away from the present, actively studies the past – history, statistics etc. (The influence of the stirrup in world history.) Has no single interest except the widespread ordering of many general facts. He clings to routines: certain drinks, hats, old rendezvous. So vague, almost seems selfish. Eats noisily. Cannot make up his mind. Procrastinations which create further misunderstandings, complications, errors. (Hamlet without the blood.)

Women are attracted to some of this, those quiet firm ones with late exasperation thresholds. He is only 30.


Mr History (2). Young skinny Englishman, grinning, who likes to correct people's grammar etc. Worked at Butlin camp in Cornwall as 'Mister History'. He'd come on to the fanfare of an ex-circus band. 'Mis-ter His-toreee!' Short bow. 'Ask me any question, any question. Ask me a date. Anyone who catches me out wins a free packet of cigarettes.'

He was fired for not 'having the right attitude'. Now lives in Philadelphia.


Bus full of pensioners on holiday crashed into a house, killing six, and bringing down a wall which revealed the body of another pensioner who had died the day before and was being laid out.


Again C. argued his belief in being strictly honest at all times. He was being rigid. She differed but could not change him. They worked together in the same office. Finally she said, 'Do you want me to be really honest to prove how wrong you are?' 'Of course,' he replied. 'You bore people with your endless talk on your BBC film scripts. You're a bore. That's being honest.'

The man began crying.

She looked into her wine-glass and tried to stop herself from crying. He got up, and came back after a while.

'I did not apologise,' she said to me.


Man to woman: 'If that baby doesn't stop bawling, I'm going up to Scotland.' (Langham Street)


One – only one – of the instruments in the Salvation Army band was dented.


When the big dog lifted his leg and pissed through the rails and down onto the window, I too wanted to climb up into the open air.


The Partitions. Mad illogical race (boredom?) over the office partitions, through glass and weak walls. Women, slipped stockings. Climbing, pushing. Style is droll, almost a race call; a rollicking effect. 'No winners.' Copulating couple on desk. A frantically clean man. Obstacles to progress. Office lamp smelling of pussy. Office is shaped like a coffin. Their names. Man pulling faces (an occupant alone). A crash through glass. The window-cleaner. Signs on wall, calendars, mirrors.

Story. A partition filled with clergymen. Another filled with doors.

'The Empire of Things.'

Restaurant in Chelsea decorated with palms, ceiling fans, bamboo, and the waiters American draft-dodgers. 'Yes, sir. This is the closest I'm getting to the tropics.'

According to C.S.: Ezra Pound lived two doors down in Langham Street, No. 48, next to the pub, in 1908. His bed took up most of the room. He wrote 'Sestina: Altafoote' there. 'Technically one of my best, though a poem on such a theme could never be important.'

Interest in all this, then a studied indifference.

As for C.S. I often want to shake his Englishness.

Indian story. The death of Nuru. Hatred is a form of love.

Driving through the countryside, scenery which is *there*, merely to see where other people live. Waste.

Edinburgh. Black buildings, rain. It seems to have a river in a valley, but looking over the bridge it's all galvanized iron, or black tracks, a vast mechanical river of railway sheds and lines – there in the centre of town.

And policemen, museum attendants, railway porters have a shy manner, especially before M. In turn, it makes me almost tentative.

Printed on the toilet paper: NOW WASH YOUR HANDS, PLEASE.

Dundee. Entire blocks of condemned buildings; a feeling that something is *wrong*. Doors slammed in the wind indicating each building's emptiness, as if I was on an inspection.

The most interesting exhibits in the Maritime Museum, Aberdeen: two elephant tusks caught in nets in the North Sea, a long time ago.

These modern Scots of all ages, bearded, arms folded, sit in cafés in dripping nylon jackets with stunned and obedient expressions, as if they've just been taken off a shipwreck.

The Corn Exchange at Leeds.

Sunday afternoon. Langham Street. A steam-roller went past, and the floors, walls and windows of the basement vibrate. Not so much the weight of the world as the looseness of the world – myself, these things.

'She was a mother of two struck dead one day at 32.'

Eyelashes: almost claws.

Dream. Close-up of filthy, fascinating shop window. Through the glass outside is the shop-keeper and a 'spy' in a grubby raincoat or some sort of runaway-man who has been given the address for the solution – his instructions for where to go next. The shopkeeper has 'a message' for him in the window among the junk. Facing him, I begin searching with my eyes too. There are weird useless objects, things out of context, unused things, and books with meaningful titles, slips of paper with phrases, advice. The shop-keeper mentions all this to the impatient man who keeps looking (and so at me) through the window. Weird advice bureau. No result.

'Movies seem to prosper in an intellectual and moral vacuum.'
— Buñuel

To take a breather, the shoe salesman held onto the door frame with one hand and leaned out like a tram conductor.

Palmeira dos Indios, Brazil, June 9, Reuters:
The Mayor of this north-eastern Brazil city has desisted from his intent of mustering a majority in the city council to repeal the law of gravity, according to press reports.

Mayor Minervo was annoyed at the law of gravity because city engineers told him it prevented their building a water tank on the steeply sloping square of the city.

When he called on the council's majority leader Jaime Guilaraes to muster the party councilmen to repeal the law, he was told it was better to leave it alone.

'We do not know whether this is a municipal

or state law and it might even be a federal law,' Guilaraes said. 'It is better not to get mixed up in this business so as not to create any problems,' he added.

His phone was dirty. He said he cleaned it with a bread roll and ate it.

He notices teeth. 'Ah, you've had a filling at the back. I noticed that.'

Story. 'Basement Notes'. Notes exchanged throughout the building, originating from the basement. Kindly be quieter . . . Please, which room are you? Arguments above. One dies. Etc.

Remembered (again): staying with T.B. during the heatwave outside Renmark in their rented wooden bungalow in the vineyard. One room was locked, never to be entered. Through the keyhole: a few weapons and relics from India, and things on the left I couldn't see.

'Thanks for the postcard,' someone said to C.S. at the end of the phone conversation. He said. 'Ohhh . . .' Not disagreeing. But he hadn't sent a card to him or anyone, and began to think this person was trying to insert himself into his life.


Burton's tomb (behind the Catholic church): the force exerted by a tent made of paradoxical material – concrete. A cross fitted absurdly above the Moslem crescent. Elsewhere weeds and rust.


Voting Communist in the council elections. I don't belong here.


English disease. A.R. had to crawl under the stage at Bristol, the oldest theatre in England. Ancient floorboards, centuries of dust and dried-out actors' spittle. Next day he came down with a disease. He had the pallor, languid hand movements and formality ('See you anon!') of the 18th century. Lassitude and a gentle looking backwards; a draining of any ambition whatsoever.


Some mornings I try hard to determine the edges of things (buildings). Naturally I then think of the difficulties encountered by Australian painters who tried to work here.

'Come to our place. We've put down new carpets.'

4.30am Two short, very sharp thumps: I was woken up. An explosion and some distance away. There was something falling on a roof nearby. Nothing else. The windows didn't rattle. Still dark, one or two people walking along the street. Nightwatchmen stood outside their doors. A herd of fire engines met in Regent Street. I looked up and saw bits of metal hanging from the top of the Post Office Tower. Near the bomb area a policewoman let me pass when I said I lived nearby. Pink-cheeked and ridiculously young.

'When we say "Time" we mean ourselves. Most abstractions are simply our pseudonyms. It is superfluous to say, "Time is scytheless and toothless". We know it. We are time.' – Cavafy

When his wife was away, he dressed in her clothes, he said. Nodding and trying to appear thoughtful, I only frowned. But then I thought: that's all right, I don't want to encourage him.

In his early thirties, but already bull-necked and red-faced: shirt striped and yellowish hair combed into stripes. All he could loudly talk about to the two young men eating with him was the stock market, how he was making a killing etc. As he repeated his successes and became more and more definite in his pronouncements they became even more servile. 'I have two brokers,' he said. 'One clever one, and one very stupid one.'

In the end he paid for his share with Luncheon Vouchers; and they split the bill precisely.

Complacent stasis in the design of British motor-cycles and the decline of the Empire – pre-Suez.

Milton, Cecil, Reg, Lance: remote-sounding names of uncles, from another generation.

P. A fast talker, answering questions before the last syllable has died, averting eyes (black-rimmed glasses, rosy cheeks) and fidgeting, his sentences come out rounded-off and confident, especially literary statements. He'd glance across for a reaction when he uttered something young or clever. He has a kind of hectic remoteness. At the same time so matter-of-fact and modest as to be exceptionally fair.

Often I see myself walking towards myself (even when I'm not walking).

Amsterdam. Long trams. Ugly men. Wide women.

At night a Dutch habit of allowing themselves to be seen illuminated in their living rooms, with no curtains. And so entire apartment blocks are subdivided and lit for display, each room containing small figures, seated or moving.

The taxi driver sounded his horn at the van stopped in front with its indicator flashing. After several minutes he opened the door and went and talked to the driver, and returned expressionless.

Bar near the docks. Sailors and young Dutchmen each with a cigarette hanging from the corner of their mouths. Man with big scar across one eye asked to 'see' the barmaid's eye-makeup, and when someone laughed asked again louder. Thin drunk in suit, drinking straight from a bottle, sang to the barmaid. Sang badly. Old woman to an untidy couple: 'Is she giving you trouble? If she is, this is what you do.' Cracked the other woman across the face. 'There, if she gives trouble, give her that.'

Rotterdam. At the museum the woman complained of a child's clogs making noise on the Kandinsky room floor.


The horizontality of the land simply enters the mind without obstacles. A tree assumes sudden, inordinate importance.


The Irishman in his room, drunk, saw his underpants moving across the floor - being taken by a rat. Jumps on them.


R.K. arguing in Piccadilly near closing time: fuzzy, inarticulate, dogmatic, all with a kind of Melbourne innocence. To meet the artist or writer is usually a disappointment.


Movement of mail. As a letter travels through the landscape at 0.38 miles per hour the consequences of its contents have already begun.


Has practised English calm to the extent of holding his mouth open, his lower lip protruding unconcerned, when taking decisive action on something.

A set of traffic lights being transported on a truck, the truck waiting for other lights to change.

I felt like confiding: I too am beginning to frown permanently, but am not necessarily unhappy.

Red hair, small dark eyes.

R.P. said he saw in L.A. a man dressed as dummy, posing motionless in a shop window. Occasionally he blinked.

Afterwards he realised something and said to his wife she was the oldest woman he had fucked. 'I suppose as long as I don't play around this will always be so.'

'. . . nations, those vast collective beings, are subject to the same laws as individuals . . . They have their childhood, they have their youth and maturity, and they have their old age, when they fall asleep on their heaped up riches.'
                                                    – Baudelaire, 1855

A bigot with body odour (window-cleaner).

His hand was broken outside a hotel – run over by a Rolls Royce. While drunk, he tried to stop it. That was how he met his wife. She was the nurse they sent around.

Scarecrows: dressed as policemen.

'Petrified good manners.'        – Kafka

Story. Man thinks he is dying and decides to tell people what he's always wanted to (but constrained by the living): writes to E., 'You're the nearest thing to a fascist I've ever met' etc., etc. Goes back to Australia to die. His friends have changed slightly towards each other. But E. hears that he hasn't died at all and goes to Aust. Etc., etc.

Holding a woman's hand while walking: it is an unusual action, when thought about.

War Museum. An exaggeration of attendants – all of military bearing, white-haired, some with ribbons and the moustache. Factual, almost clinical descriptive labels on the flamethrowers. Insufficient horror in the many small photographs, unlike the present ones printed every day from Vietnam. The emphasis is on the young pilots waiting in deck-chairs on the grass, their spotted cravats a feature; or else the immaculate famous commander inspecting troops somewhere. Shaking hands. Of the bomb and the ovens, the Imperial War Museum has assigned an arm's width to Hiroshima, nothing on the exterminated Jews. An entire display case devoted to the RAF breaking the walls of a prison holding Resistance members in France, killing half the guards and allowing 70 prisoners to escape, losing two bombers.

After sacrifice the necessity of myth. Imagery so chosen accumulates into something adventurously pro-war.


Woman's unusually fat fingers. I wanted to avoid their touch when she gave change.


Oxford. Strolling through the ancient quadrangles etc. and actively resisting being encrusted with tradition. Blowing my nose, talking loudly.

Forest with russet leaves as if recently devoured by an Australian bushfire.

Today I bought de Chirico's *Hebdomeros*. Because a painter had written a novel. And I saw 'Melbourne' in the second sentence.

Study of two people from the back only. Possible.

*The Times:*

Mr Leonard Kavanagh, described by neighbours as introverted, lay dead for between 12 and 18 months in his London flat before being found by police yesterday. Mr Kavanagh, believed to be a former wall-of-death-motor-cyclist, was aged about 50 and lived alone in the flat above the chemist's shop in Willesden Lane, Willesden.

The owner of the shop and flat, Mr Henry Bliss, said Mr Kavanagh had to pass through the shop to get to his front door, but he had a door at the back, which he used more frequently. 'There was no reason to be suspicious because Mr Kavanagh was not the sort of person to be seen around very much,' Mr Bliss said. He last saw his tenant about two years ago. Etc., etc.

He said he painted his dog green and took a photograph of it to get a refund from Kodak.

On leaving the army 40 years ago, he vowed 'that as long as I lived I would never do another stroke of physical exercise in any shape or form'. (Aged 81)

Story. 'To Whom It May Concern'. 'Let me correct the impression I made last night. I am not . . .' etc. Corrects each person's view of him, revealing himself.

Some animals – a minority of horses, for example – must also have poor eyesight.

Two Texans came with their daughter. He walked in tall and tanned with a camera in his hand already fitted with flash.

Paris. 24.12.71. Staggering bureaucracy, an extension of the baroque, like the proliferation of gargoyles and caryatids in French architecture.

A sociological difference between the deck-chairs in London parks and those in Paris of ornate wrought iron: the former are for people resting, the latter for hard, aware types.

Signs in French metro carriages requesting people to stand for (in this order):
1. People injured in war.
2. Civilians who are blind or injured.
3. Pregnant women.

Homeless men lying in rows over the metro gratings for the warm air.

Fairground, Paris. Life-size photos of strippers in 3-D followed me as I walked past. And young Africans from France's colonies happily ramming pimply French girls in the dodgem-cars.

At least Sartre, Debray etc. commit themselves on the streets instead of penning a letter to *The Times*.

Grenoble. Tennis courts filled with snow.

Emerging from three floors of Francis Bacon at the Grand Palais it was the streets, traffic and trees of the bright-aired everyday world that seemed less 'real'. 'The image must be twisted if it is to make a renewed assault on the nervous system . . . and that is the peculiar difficulty of painting today.'                                    – Bacon

Story. 'Ears, Diseases of'. Perplexed tone. 'For some time I have had trouble with my ears (you have troubles of your own etc., but . . . )' . . . deposits (words), irritations. These ears apparently have taken too much in. Only wants to hear a few things for the rest of his life.

At C.M.'s flat near Hampstead, he kept the TV on during dinner, glancing at it. After all he was Britain's leading surrealist.

'I tell you, Mrs Fuse, when you're silly, you're silly. But when you're mental, people make allowances.'

An Australian, Roy . . . was badly hurt when a woman landed on him after falling out of a building in Oxford Street. Novel here, not a story. He saved her life.

25 Campden Hill Gardens. Rooms with natural light, as if I am no longer 'struggling'. The luxury of a bay window. Large brown wardrobes, ticking clock with loud chimes activated by pulleys and loops of wire, foxed watercolours in ancient frames. On the shelf beneath the lampshade a life-sized plaster bust of her lover, an ageing businessman she met in India, now in Yorkshire, retired – unable to leave his heavy-drinking wife. From all sides an association which commands interest and respect. (Sets of his clothes, including shoes, in the wardrobes.) Old English plates mounted on the wall, among brass objects – out of place trophies – from an alien place, India, add to the atmosphere of patience.

9.9.72. Running uphill at one a.m. past John McDouall Stuart's house I felt (a few weeks before 31) my breasts wobbling like a woman's. Slight feeling of entering a new bodily age.

Strange seeing the blank, sedentary appearance of the explorer's house.

Told on phone of R.K.'s murder (woman, breadknife, St. Kilda Rd). Thickness of throat; then unwanted feeling of lack of surprise.

Certain people certainly live longer.

In 1801 Benjamin West and two other painters took delivery of James Legg, a Chelsea pensioner hanged for murdering a fellow old soldier. They needed him for research purposes. While his body was still pliable, they stuck it on a cross and made a plaster cast which went to the Academy schools as evidence of what a crucified body really looks like. Arms spread, the crucifixion is the image of Prometheus bound to his rock, of Icarus poised to fly . . . of vermin tacked to a fence to dry out.

T.S. He speaks like his appearance: strong-jawed, positive, thrusting, but reasonable. And it's no laughing matter. It's too reasonable.

The lamp flickered and came on above his head as if he had a sudden bright idea.

Battered ex-boxer went to Sydney in the 1930s for three fights and lost all three. The arches of the Harbour Bridge had not joined. He had wondered how the cars had crossed. Broken nose, cauliflower ears, now selling lengths of cloth at Petticoat Lane (mound of cauliflower ears on the next stall).

Invited to play table-tennis in a mental home, they went into a room where the table was surrounded by rows of quietly-seated patients. But then a patient directed them, like a traffic policeman, halting them, beckoning invisible traffic, then waving them on.

'To prove the existence of yesterday' – suggested aim of the writer (Arakawa).

I sat on the pavement table at the coffee shop in George Street behind Sotheby's. In the window, facing me, the Chinese Porcelain Expert worked on a catalogue; along the street, to my left, two men loaded in slow motion a grand piano onto a truck. A middle-aged man entered the shop carrying a large square envelope; I stood up and decided to follow him. It was two o'clock . . .

*Aphrodisiac Jacket* (Dali)
*Definite Refusal of a Demand for a Kiss*
*Method of Reading Extreme Altitudes* (R.H. Goddard, 1919)
*Catastrophe Theory*

He still keeps a horse and cart 'because grass can't go on strike'.

*The Charms of Dynamite*
*Lies, All Lies*
*The Brain of Einstein*
*The Waste of Daylight*
*In Advance of the Broken Arm* (Duchamp)
*Missionary of Insolence*
*Paraphernalia*

Constant contest: against cynicism, sourness, instinct to put others and things down.

'I was always very critical, liable to too easy a contempt. I think this is something my father gave me. My father was a defeated man: I think contempt was all he could teach me, and I was contaminated by this.'           – V.S. Naipaul

Story: Begin: 'Nevertheless . . .'

Dymphna Martyr, patron saint of lunatics.

This Englishman (J.G.) who led an expedition in Afghanistan tramping across other people's land, yet when he saw from the footpath I had a visitor would not come in.

A story full of deliberate mistakes.

At the office someone said, 'You look as if you're dying.'

Foolishly, I felt almost pleased.

At the Paris cemetery C.S. saw two separate graves of a man and wife, and from each headstone emerged an arm and hand to clasp each other across space.

41 Royal Crescent. At the other end directly opposite, Bridget Riley's house and studio, unlike all the others, is lit with fluorescent lighting.

In Holland Park tube station the wall clock was bandaged with white tape obliterating the hands, hiding the 'stopped' time. It was a 'sick' clock, or 'sick' time.

Home, she was removing the covers off the chairs. Under one cover was an old brown cushion. She almost wanted to cry, was depressed all day.

Washing up, she suddenly imagined her 3-year-old daughter walking in the door behind her – as a 70-year-old woman. It was a vision. She 'froze', unable to turn around and began to cry.

Thanatology and thaumaturgy.

Albert Hall concert: contact lenses reflected in the dark boxes the way the eyes of foxes and spiders shine in the spotlight.

Human cuckoo, one-eyed British painter in old overcoat down to the ankles, who always lived in another person's room, depositing himself. A series of bed-sitters across London. He took a job cleaning lavatories and made them so spotless he hated people using them: he'd put up signs, OUT OF ORDER. Who had a violent temper, yet was passive. Destroyed a painting at anyone's suggestion.

After he read of his obituary – a body mistaken – he began, after ten years, to paint again.

A room filled with clergymen, all facing more or less the one direction.

'When I look at a scene in the country, I see a signature in the lower right-hand corner.'

– Steinberg

A man who wants to save someone's life. He constantly thinks about it.

In the last twelve months my hands have begun to look like middle-aged hands, and in the mirror my face skin is coarser, the nose no longer a young man's. I look worried – vertical line in forehead – but it is failing eyesight, I tell myself.

From the fifth floor, the white-haired man on the ground appeared to be having a fit. But the bicycle was black and in shadow; I hadn't seen it as he contorted himself trying to climb on.

He left his wife and five children for a younger woman. 'The wife was a Scotswoman who literally counted the matches.' After three years he returned. His eldest daughter was pregnant and unmarried. His presence is tolerated by his family, but ignored. 'Who is that?' – the figure making tea. 'Oh, him.' Allowed to 'exist', but never spoken to. Then after several years he got throat cancer, and he could no longer speak.

He wrote bitter notes. 'You fucking whore,' he scribbled. He would leave such notes on the table, on the sideboard, in the kitchen. The illegitimate daughter grew up among this. My friend, who was her father, was confronted by the old mother. 'You now owe June £573.35.'


The sweeper in Bombay woken up to squat and clean the vomit on the floor while the party continued. Whites of his eyes.


Bare branches in bad weather scratch at the sky as if it were a pane of glass.


The subtle sunsets begin at 4.30pm long grey slashes – washes – like a watercolourist cleaning the brush, edges stained in pink.

And white trails from jets, curving and intersecting, the sky a vast snowfield of show-off skiers. Entirely British in its softness, slowness, subtlety: none of the spectacular violence and heat of the tropical sunsets.


I went to press my ear-lobe with my thumb but missed it entirely. Odd feeling. I was walking in the street.

Coming towards me a man leading a dog (Holland Park Ave). It was straining to the left, at right angles, making his arm point down at 45 degrees. From a distance the leash was invisible so the man appeared to be jerking the dog by pointing with his forefinger.

Among the survivors of the Ethiopian hijacking was a group of British bird-watchers. Bullets, grenades, legs blown off. 'I did a lot of nothing,' said Mr MacIntosh, a bird-watcher. 'One did what one could to help.' Whereas, the American: 'I said to myself this is it.' He saw a woman hijacker crawling down the aisle. 'A security guard was right behind her. He pumped her head so full of lead she couldn't pick it up any more.'

Story. Bed-ridden, dying (?) manufacturer of 'microphones and loudspeakers' is speaking into one of his microphones (model no . . .) and loud-speakers, confessing his doubts, regrets, anxi-eties, problems of conscience etc. Broadcasting his fears.

The blindnesses and other troubles (deaths) microphones and loudspeakers have caused.

She said reincarnation must be so because more and more people are looking like dogs, cats, snakes, hippos, bulls, cows, and their behaviour is violent, animal-like. And because there are progressively more deaths, she went on, there are more reincarnations walking the streets and 'seen out in the country'.

Through the network of black branches the full moon looked like an illuminated clock. The origin of the clock-face?

With his loose sole it seemed as if his foot was talking. So I paid attention.

Marrakesh, 23.12.72. Again, the altogether larger skies of the underdeveloped country. The many small motor-cycles, invariably with a passenger: a woman in borka, her cheek pressed against his back. Ochre (the walls): ancient colour. For all the apparent poverty, trees in the street nevertheless laden with oranges. A beggar being pushed along by two friends – doubly short, a dwarf, without legs.

Black soap in buckets, like grease.

Boy pestering to be a guide, when asked if he attended school: 'I could teach a teacher.'

Good-humoured people, even the hustlers. The bad-tempered ones happen to be the mule drivers.

Drinking mint tea from glass cups and the feeling of being somewhere else.

Three or four staring men seated in cafés, eating a stew, wearing rough woollen kaftans.

Rotten (or solitary) teeth.

Beginning to dislike these places. I am inquisitive and they are accommodating me.

At the tombs of the Saadian kings there is never the name of the dead person, only a different design. Courageous anonymity.

The Berber guide in the museum – jet black in a dark brown, hooded kaftan. After saying something bold or answering a silly question he would give a soft laugh, a form of discretion or nervousness. It became like the patter of feet in the dark museum and I began to like him immeasurably.

In the cafés the fluorescent tubes and the garish blue walls are an instinctive attempt to reproduce the light and space of the surrounding desert.

Familiar gum trees in and around Marrakesh, as in New Delhi.

Prospective buyer testing the balls of sheep and a goat. Men haggling over sheep's heads in the abattoir. Dogs and small boys standing bare-foot in blood filling the 'gutters'.

Stony road to Amizmiz.
A camel ploughing.
Mud villages embedded in bare hills slide across the mind and into cubism.

Horse beneath golden trees, the leaves falling like money.

Few police, more soldiers.

Atlas Mountains: jagged, streaked with snow. They attract clouds as heavy as suspended boulders.

A clean garrison town, Onarzazate. At its far end the ancient fort of five storeys in pressed mud.

The feeling of being on the edge of the Sahara and wanting to press on into the emptiness. Dusk.

Irritation at what I imagined to be the general clumsiness of the others, even M.: caution and social duty.

The road empty. Below, an oasis at dusk: dark green, with wet squares of mercury, a few flat buildings, palms. Ahead the boulder-styled clouds tinged pink in the mauve lower sky. The vast sky. Brown land. The silent peaks. No movement anywhere. Day merging into night: a staining of the senses.

The bored belly-dancer.

Out in the desert in the middle of nowhere a cluster of brightly dressed boys playing soccer.

The Islamic dome which originated in these barren landscapes is surely an imitation of the great sky where there is more colour and often more activity than on the earth.

So happy I laughed when anyone spoke.

*Churel* (Hindi) – ghost of a woman who died in childbirth – haunts lonely roads.

The earth was camel-covered.

How, as the plane climbs, scientific perspective is reduced until it is shown to be artificial. But standing on the earth it is the only 'logical' way to see, record and imply distance.

From the air, the viewpoint is from a position of near-nothingness: illimitable space.

\* \* \*

New Year's day, 1973. Heavy fog. Muffles the sound of traffic and other feelings.

With little warning I read a novel of commanding force, intelligence: *The Erl King*. Through his thoughts the author himself (Michel Tournier) almost becomes the most interesting character.

Time is limitless, doesn't wear, is perpetual, doesn't vary. It cannot be said to exist?

Story. Film over speaker. Someone steps in front of a film; addresses an audience on stage. The film ('underground' film) stops, starts up again, interrupting him. He keeps talking as images from his life wander over his face and body. He attempts an explanation (of his presence, of his life), but his established, recorded life is superimposed.
Audience. Battle in projection room.

Gazing in the mirror, and continuing. Sudden disgust at this.

Letter in *The Times*:
Sir, For more than 20 years I have kept an accurate daily record of my outdoor walking

mileage, and for the past 20 years I find that it totals 72,721 miles, and thus produces an annual average of 3,636 miles or nearly 10 miles per day. My best year was 1972 with annual, monthly and weekly maxima respectively of 5,337, 503 and 120 miles.

I am sure that these figures must be and have been exceeded by many people quite often, but consideration of them has caused me to wonder what might be the ground covered on foot in a lifetime. Half a million miles (100 years at 5,000 miles for each) would seem to me to be more than anyone could have achieved and even half that distance would represent a formidable undertaking. At the age of 60, and without accurate records for the first 35 of them, I estimate that I have walked about 122,000 miles to date.

Are there, however, any recorded instances of very high mileages covered by individuals over a lifetime or other lengthy period?

A musical forehead: staff lines almost numbering five and a bar line had become impressed above his nose. At the bus stop he was humming.

Sign in shop window (in pencil): NO MORE EXCUSES.

According to A.J.P. Taylor, Lenin published 10 million words.

Working in the trench, the boy tossed a mug of tea across the footpath, at my feet. An accident, but he looked at me challengingly. I smiled and tried to shake my head sadly.

The married man who called his wife 'Bunny' and his younger mistress 'Rabbit'.

The last time they met, R.'s mother showed them slides of her all-consuming passion – her varieties of cactus. 'She had a special glasshouse built. She was always independent.'

Royal Crescent, W11 . . . 'was laid out in 1841 . . . and so the name was partly patriotic in origin. But its main function was an "advertising" name intended to attract buyers to the new development.' Mister History: '1841? Wasn't that when the first zinc battery was invented? And some other important thing happened. I'll look it up, if you like.'

Women are somehow repelled by H.R.'s wretchedness. Sensing that he fixes onto men.

'The Northern Territory.' I like its sound and its appearance on the page.

Lines around her mouth and jaw curved like wet hairs.

A group is 'holding' Ayers Rock against invasion or assaults on various sensibilities, including provincialism. Defections.

Interesting word, 'screen'.

As he was about to pay, A. asked, 'Just a minute. These aren't South African grapes, are they?' Cockney stallholder: 'No, guv. No niggers have touched these.'

Story. 'A,B,C,D,E,F etc.' 'I sit here selecting from these letters (26 shapes), pressing a finger down to repeat the shape on paper, until I form a word.'

'I am writing a story, a pile of letters arranged

in a certain order. Etc. I am selecting letters to form words . . .'

The letter (or image of it) appears on the sheet of paper.

The word 'dog' does not bite (James).

TREE: and I see one, green.

Language his only certainty.


My wife is shaving her legs with Nigerian razor blades, helping the Third World.


Woman in sandwich bar: 'The blouse I bought was petrol-coloured.'


Rough man to woman poking her tongue out at him: 'You're not going to put that back in your mouth, are you?'


Graffiti, Notting Hill: HELP STAMP OUT QUICKSAND.

Normally I would have smiled.


During the building of the Kensington Hilton some gas cylinders exploded, and the houses in Royal Crescent met the blast in a perfect semi-circle. R.G-W.: 'Many of the windows broke all around the crescent. There was a lull, then a second sound of breakages as people swept objects off their side-tables for the insurance.'

'Funny sort of day' – introductory words of a young overweight man in pub, in need of company.

This interest, for no apparent reason, in the way women decorate themselves: lipsticks, rings, bangles, necklaces, ankle bracelets, not their clothes.

Official rent-assessor went through each room speaking into a tape-recorder: 'Some of the things I see would make your hair stand on end.'

Black and white photographs of British politicians recently passed over or dead, Gaitskell, Bevan, Chamberlain etc., even Macmillan, exude in their dress the *mustiness* of the past. It's depressing thinking of that lost time; whereas figures of the New World, Eisenhower, Stevenson, Roosevelt, even Truman, have a certain freshness, openness.

During the war his friends erected an enormous tent in the darkness on the parade ground in front of him while he was half-asleep on guard duty. Sergeant: 'Were you on sentry duty last night?' 'Sir!' 'Then what d'you think that is there?'

Really all these understated (i.e. overstated) signs of class begin to look like so many relics, even when brand new (the Rolls Royces, the discreet pin-stripes, pheasants in the windows, watch chains and shooting jackets – forms of spreading darkness).

The new decimal currency: paucity of design, paucity of purchasing power.

'He leapt a good ten feet into the air.'

Often he gets out at the station and I walk down Holland Park Ave behind or almost alongside him. Several times I have almost asked how his face became hideously burnt. He cannot smile.

'. . . the ship *Argo* of which the Argonauts gradually changed each part, so that they finally had a new ship without having to change its name or form.'

While he was crawling around and being shot at in Vietnam his grandmother sent him a map of the proposed underground trainlines for Adelaide.

Maroon carpet on the stairs of the flat of the loudly talkative (firm but decent) Englishwoman and her lawyer husband who seizes upon (with a certain triumph of memory) topographical details around where they live. The furnishings, the books on the shelves, their ideas, even their appearance, have a strange air of practical back-wardness. Lift-well encased in thick opaque glass and cream paint.

Sounded like a tram (accelerating truck's whining axle).

'All right? O.K!'

Not the river of prose, but a flood-plain of sen-sations: alertness and beauty from all directions, and all depths. A marvellous curiosity transmit-ted. Ideas, laughter. Amazed at my complacency:

to think I hadn't begun reading this most complete novel (Proust), even one day earlier.

Opened the newspaper to find nothing after p.3 but blank pages. Slight alarm or incomprehension then thought about other things.

After repeated cross-examinations, one of Alexander II's assassins finally said, 'Sometimes history needs a push.'

G. Steiner: he was like an ugly violinist who becomes transformed by the production of words and ideas. Arrived clutching an absurd-looking tiny briefcase.

The tidal attraction of breasts: liquid fullness, related to the moon? And in shadow one side of her cleavage appeared in eclipse.

About to be married, and slender. Both had loud, confident voices and the well-rounded vowels (were in a position not to care what others heard, what others thought). Only about 23, yet she said: 'No darling, if we choose a pine bed now, it's not the sort of thing we'd want to pass onto our children. Future generations would not want a *pine* bed. We must think of that, darling.'

He listened with his arms folded and a blank look (prematurely striped tie). 'I see, darling. You're right.'


'Look at him asking questions again. You've found a way to be popular.'


Some things which are part of the world are actually peculiar substances. Grass, for example.


The footpath and gutters asserting themselves: coming forward at me, in their absolute essence. Other days I don't notice.


Children born after 20 July 1969 have a different view of themselves within the universe. Arriving after a man has stood on the moon, they begin on a higher plane of assumptions.


She laughed to reveal her throat. But that was all.

Two years ago at a café in Edinburgh a bony
goat-bearded man, about 50, at a table full of
vocal people. With him a young serene woman
with long straight hair, peaches-and-cream com-
plexion. He appeared unusually alive; an Ezra
Pound in the north. And he participated in a
way that suggested greater knowledge or experience. He wore a green shirt and tie.

G.G. in London mentioned a friend of his, an
American artist living on Skye, was visiting.
Foolish pride at people's amazement as I
described him down to his crooked teeth,
woollen tie, serene girlfriend at elbow.

'But it would be interesting to meet this man
who made such an impression across a crowded
room in Edinburgh.'


In court on a sexual offences charge and asked
why he had been in the public lavatory with that
man, the Cypriot replied, 'It was my mother's
birthday and she's in Athens.'


This hirsute generation: anything to do with
being between wars?


Story. Portrait formed by traces, preserved.
A mirror he used – 'this had registered his
image'. His writing on blotter – 'unfortunately

137

upside-down'. Telephone with dusty cord – 'it was through these wires, through the copper, springs and plastic that he gave his instructions'. 'What were his instructions?' 'His breath travelled along these wires, his personality.' 'Electricity proved his existence?' 'If you like, yes.' Etc. Woman: 'What did his voice sound like?' 'Ah, let me attempt an imitation.' 'Portrait of Electricity.' (Arakawa.)

Shape of his shadow preserved in outline, for all time.

The necessity of rulers (yardsticks).

Lagophthalmus. Unable to close eyes. A nightmare.

In the paper-mill women who worked crouched under the long machines in total din (not even the radio can be heard), in heat and boredom, nevertheless dislike being moved. They – and not the males – according to the foreman – develop a possessiveness towards their machines, which have little personality quirks and weaknesses almost as living things.

Rolls of soft pink and blue paper, twelve feet

high, stacked to the ceiling: ready for defecating giants.

Irritation at crowd behind Bond Street applauding as the Queen Mother stepped out of her Daimler (double-parked). Their distracted, washed-out expressions as they dispersed, satisfied. Their clapping was a language.

The sighting of someone exclusive does not necessarily constitute an 'experience'.

Paris, Easter 1973. At the Coupole an old man with long white hair emptied ballpoint pens on the table and tried to sharpen them with a razor blade.

Through the window at the Louvre, a courtyard and a goldfish pond with a small boy fishing. Strange feeling of relief.

Stunted plump woman seated on a very high stool, copying a Rubens. She wore a leopard-skin hat.

Multiple vanity of the exhibitionist surveying the crowd admiring his fine copy of a de la Tour, just finished. Some began photographing him with his copy in front of the original; and on the easel was his photograph, taken in 1928, standing alongside his fine copy of the *Mona Lisa* in front of the original – this photograph was also included in the photograph, a copy of another copy depicting another copy.

Why so satisfied? Over all those years his copying appeared to have improved only marginally.

Typically the windows on Paris buses are much larger (inviting participation) than the London double-deckers (which encourage a looking-down).

The wiry landscape of France.

Walking around the base of Flavigny, along faint paths. Violets, small birds and crows at odds with the cold; ivy strangling trees.

Towards the top, two red squirrels jumping from tree to tree. The sound before that was a cuckoo.

Light snow began to fall.

Village idiots sit on stools out in the open. Hunchbacks and figures with club-feet too, as if they have each been assigned specific tasks.

So riddled with shrapnel the Gothic cathedral looks splattered with grey mud. Rouen.

Dense clouds like cement smoke.

Woman aged 63: 'I've wanted to do three things in my life and now I'm too old for any of them. Write a book, paint a picture, and play the saxophone.'

In Grosvenor Square in the rain a motor-cycle had fallen off its stand and its billowing water-proof cover looked like a trapped, gasping rider.

'I'd like you to meet my eldest. He's got a big mouth like his father.'

Succubus.

*The Times*:

Dubai, June 15. – An Englishman rescued from the Atlantic off West Africa told reporters today of how he jumped from a ship into the ocean after thinking he saw his dead wife in the water.

Mr Lawrence John Ellis, aged 31, said he stowed away in a container ship in Liverpool with a friend on May 15 because he was anxious to get to Australia where his wife had died last December.

He and his companion were allowed to work in the ship after being discovered, but he 'became very depressed' thinking about his wife.

'Nothing could stop me remembering my wife that night of May 21 . . . As I walked on deck I believed I could see her in the water beckoning to me . . . So certain was I that I got two lifebelts, lashed them together, and dived into the sea. I quickly surfaced and began to search for my wife. The water was ice cold and I saw the lights of the ship disappearing.'

Mr Ellis said that with the coming of the dawn and the sun, he thought he was going to die.

Badly sunburned he was about to give up hope of rescue, but he saw one or two ships and waved. They did not see him so he decided to strike out for the shore. He was 100 miles off the coast of Guinea.

Finally, after 10 hours in the water, he was

seen and picked up by an Italian tanker *Esso Augusta*.


To be a barman (unable to have strong opinions).


The German words for 'history' and 'story' are the same.


A man who lives alone in a cluttered (?) room falls seriously ill and, when he eventually emerges, finds the other rooms of his house have changed – with different, unknown furniture, objects and colour. Unrecognisable except for minor touches.


He followed her about the museum without meaning to until they stood together in front of the same pictures, like an old couple.


Actually, it is strange to think of ships travelling on the waterways between land (and the way they are fastened to the earth by ropes).

A ship named after someone wanders away from the person, but is still connected as they sleep.

Corrugated iron from the air. East Africa, etc.


Talking on the phone to certain people she brushes back her hair with one hand.


Touching my nose. Just checking.


The leader of the successful Italian expedition to Everest placed a plaque representing the Madonna and Child on the summit. He sent a telegram to the Pope. The very idea of this. He must have thought about it and decided on this in Rome. Then selected it – the right Madonna. Then packed it for the climb. Then always having the lead climber carry it. Taking it up. Finally the moment of planting it on the highest point on earth. Why?

Tenzing, a Buddhist, also put something there in 1953 (flowers and food).


Stories. 'Camouflage'.


In order to gain rest, to 're-charge', a businessman is driven home each night in a hired ambulance. He could lie down and sleep for . . . 39 minutes.

144

She became so depressed she covered the fish bowl in the lounge with a tea-towel.

Story. Two people approaching an 'intersection', a collision course (not necessarily physical) without knowing it. Each one making unwitting adjustments in behaviour, including movements, as they approach the split second. Under certain circumstances: determinism. *In Advance of the Broken Arm*.

Literary editor on the telephone (accompanied by 'museum' echo): 'We have only one rule here, Mr B. We'd rather you didn't employ the pronoun "I".'

Story. 'Self-portrait with Flowers'. Begin: 'There are private and perverse acts, or disciplines, let us say, practised by the most normal men which the imagination, even the most practised literary one, cannot conceive. An incident is reported in the daily newspaper; sometimes a brief paragraph. The reader can only lower the page amazed.

'The case of Edward Knott, now that it is published here, will no doubt prompt writers of fiction to offer quick and easy explanations. Yet Knott's behaviour is surely outside normal psychology . . .'

*A Proposal for Correcting the English Tongue* (Swift).

Stentorophonic Story. Loud in style, loud characters, loud voices.

'London has fewer flies than any other region in the country. The average London household can muster only 0.9 of a fly per day, while in East Anglia the figure is 5.7 – the highest in the country . . .

'The methods of counting the flies are straightforward enough. All over the country men sit in rooms with a pencil and paper and tick off flies as they see them.

'The trouble is, though, that one fly looks very much like another, and there is the danger that the same one might be counted more than once.'

His uncommercial patience. Like a horse. It was his most attractive quality.

As soon as I smile I feel it, and immediately wonder whether to adjust, more or less.

Mister Buick had a wood-yard. He sold split wood, coal and coke, and pot-bellied stoves. During the summer he had nothing to do.

Two Headache Experts.

Competition to see who can become the worst soldier.

Pick three words in the dictionary at random, and write 'notes' (stories) or things they remind of: anecdotes, propositions etc.

Priest gave the sermon under a live volcano.

Interrupt fast-moving story with notes: 'Idea for a story'.

Covering my mouth with the back of my hand while listening as if determined to suppress the urge to contribute additional words.

The Offshore Fund, now bankrupt, had a tough Cuban (cigar-smoking) sales manager. Every salesman who sold in one week £100,000 worth of bonds he made a lieutenant; those who sold £150,000 he made a captain; those who sold £250,000 he made a colonel; and so on, publicly ranking his salesmen, until the rank of general was reached – selling £1,000,000. The 'general' was then photographed in colour, in an 18th-century general's uniform, and put on the cover of the staff magazine.

Picking mushrooms along the edge he slipped and fell 163 feet onto rocks. He fell off England, and lost his identity.

Often I feel like running excitedly. But I keep walking.

G. met her at a party. G., who normally talks non-stop, listened as she talked for 20 minutes. When she stopped, he asked her if she would marry him. She said yes. Next week her father sent them a microwave oven from New York.

In a bus or the tube I am torn between the necessity to read and knowing that I would become 'more observant' if I looked around.

Proust's way of employing not one simile but three or even four strung together, more and more extreme, following his thoughts as they spread in a coral growth of expansion and qualification from an action, mood or place recalled.

The spherical density of the plane tree, formed by the leaves, had been emptied. On the ground the leaves lay in a long flat shape.

A church-goer (Adelaide) arrived to find another woman had mistakenly just done the flowers. She tossed them all out and began again. My mother.

F. Bacon has also given a twist to his own appearance by combing his hair high at the sides and back at an eye-catching angle, and pouting his mouth. Pale skin, almost as if he wore make-up. Seen on Davies Street.

*The Times*:

Neighbours sympathised with Mrs Violet Blackholly when she said her husband had left her in 1963, an inquest at Walthamstow, East London, was told yesterday. But last week the skeleton of her husband was found in an upstairs

bedroom at Mrs Blackholly's house in Lidding-
ton Road, Stratford, London.

Yesterday Det. Inspector Charles Farquhar
told the inquest: 'Mrs Blackholly was the type of
person who hoarded everything she obtained.'

Returning an open verdict on Mr William
Blackholly, aged 73, Dr Harold Price, the
coroner, said: 'This is an incredible story, which
a coroner rarely comes across in his career. The
evidence of eccentricity is strong and it would
seem this elderly woman kept all her possessions.' Etc.

'The practice of art is antichrist.'          – Blake

I still like to imagine I 'suffered' in India. A form
of superiority.

Story. Every few years selected observers are
given a demonstration in the tomb in Moscow
that Lenin is not a wax model (or something). An
official tweaks Lenin's nose, shows birthmarks
etc. Fine example of d. materialism.

Lenin lies in a lounge suit, like a lawyer or
dentist. His feet appear to be missing – shorter.
Signs of the continuing shoe shortage in Moscow
etc.

Small interrelated group of observers.

Obituary:

H.E.J. writes; 'I would like to add a few personal notes on your excellent obituary of my old friend and C-in-C, ACM Sir Robert Foster, affectionately known throughout the service as "Pussy".

'He in fact had few cat-like qualities except his ability to strike sharply and suddenly if angered by something he disliked – particularly pomposity in any form.' Etc.

According to Morgenstern, all seagulls should be called Emma.

I continue to feel sympathy for petty thieves.

Dilapidated dumb-waiter.

After each sip of beer, he rolled his lips back. Unnecessarily.

Title. 'Infantile Paralysis.'

She was alone about ten yards in front; yet when I crossed the street she was level.

Breathing so heavily, I began to follow it rather than the words he was coming out with.

Stubbing out a cigarette as if she was killing an insect.

Sometimes 'Australia' appears to me as all rocks (dry, hot).

The peculiar ordinariness of the British – on the channel ferry. Their bland, practical nature: eating their own food in the lounge, sensible clothing etc.

Belgium. Straight roads which suggest getting-some-where-fast, unlike the small forever-winding British roads.

The exceptionally modern house with a thatched roof.

At the border France immediately displays the casual untidiness of a larger country.

Village near Reims called Void. Ghost village? Unpleasant feeling of futility while travelling – until something out of the ordinary comes before my eyes.

A landscape modified – scarred, pitted, broken walls, and craters and earth mounds – by waves of history, undergoing a slow recovery. Strange feeling of stillness now (near Fiestiux).

Iron windmills as in Australia, except with blades shattered from the war.

Rusting iron crosses. War produces rust.

How do people change even if they have 'seen it all'?

White crosses cover the hillside (Verdun) in mathematical rows like vineyards. Soldiers are drilled into disciplined ranks, rows of fighting men. In battle the geometry is violently broken – the regiment gassed, exploded, scattered into chaotic fragments. Afterwards their remains are returned to regimented rows, the military cemetery, to 'bear witness'.

As if, after all, order came about through war; a return to order.

Even the car junkyards are neat, the wrecks arranged in precise rows (Switzerland).

Milan. Melodramatic motor-cyclists. Historic conversationalists on pavements, under columns, seated at café tables.

In the Galleria a madman sang, walking along, his voice echoing. And people laughed good-naturedly at him and glanced at others (also laughing). Following him, a priest winked at me.

The painted-up doll at the restaurant, who'd had the same table every evening for eight years. 'Oh, some Australians sat at my table about three years ago.' She stroked my arm. 'You have pleasant skin.' She owned a clothing shop, selling among other things, underwear to men.

Roadside-workers wearing brief bathers.

The hearse with coffin doing 90mph on the autostrada.

Venice. Senses from previous experience are unprepared. The Grand Canal sparkling in the sun carries such a weight of water, a broad curving street flooded to a great depth: not even Turner or Canaletto suggest the mass of liquid – their canals are surface. And boats instead of cars, pedestrians and traffic lights. Aside from a few footsteps and voices the only sound is the thick chug of boats.

German in plus-fours asked me to hold his camera. Its concentrated weight felt like a pistol.

Woman seated on a chair inside the Jewish ghetto. She had a black eye and bandages.

Slightly tatty funeral barge. Of the four men assisting the funeral director one wore brown suede boots with his black uniform, another had his jacket off, for it was warm – he wore a khaki shirt. They had delivered the coffin on a spidery traymobile. Reclining on the grass was a drunk in a panama hat and slippers. He kept muttering. Inside the church he leaned against the holy-water stand and repeated what the priest was saying until people turned around. The funeral director remembered something – there were not enough water taxis – and he ran up to a bridge, satchel under his arm, to telephone for more. A small dog began yelping and biting at his ankles. Everyone laughed, even the funeral director, who was forced to slow down to a walk.

When the service was over, the men around their barge dropped their cigarettes, put on their coats and new solemn expressions, and went into the church. They came out struggling with the coffin, the funeral director flitting around making a path for the weeping next-of-kin. The church bells began ringing loudly, above, in a sort of momentous confusion.

'Urbino's worth seeing. It's where the safety pin was invented.'

Strapped to his chair, the village idiot began escaping by rocking it.

Priests in Italy seem to be uglier than the more humble-looking English minister.

Asked for directions the old man seated by the roadside stood up groping for M.'s hand and pointing – he was blind. Two village women in black laughed.

Florence. The receptionist at the small hotel wore an eyeshade and concentrated on painting a small landscape in oils with the aid of a special lamp rigged up, and didn't want to be disturbed.

First thing I saw as I reached the top of the Duomo after climbing 464 steps was the word AUSTRALIA scratched in the marble.

Smiling with affection at Uccello's obsession with scientific perspective.

Searching for faults in *David*. It became unnatural.

Entering Pisa, I resolved to spend the several hours in the town without allowing the leaning tower to enter my vision. An aesthetic act, part protest. 'Did you go to Pisa?' 'Yes.' 'Did you see the leaning tower?' 'No.' But in the last few minutes the others in the car tricked me and my eye filled with the circular thing standing in lawn at a crazy angle. At my unspeakable anger, only laughter, which seemed equally foolish.

Refinery in a valley, like an exposed radio set.

Completed the first eleven 'Huebler' exercises as landscape between Florence and Genoa passed.

Front wheels squeaking like forest birds.

Geneva. Its splendid rushing river, dark green.

Throughout Italy and France the same faces in medieval and Renaissance paintings can be seen moving about outside in the streets, the markets, behind the wheels of cars. By now only small variations operate within a set of established conditions. Has the Australian face arrived yet? So far it has settled on the long jaw, often with a small mouth, jug ears. A long face, solid bones, strong teeth.

(Story of man – not a woman – who decides not to see his face for 20 years. Constructs his life around this idea. Then accidentally sees it after seven. Tricked (by a woman?).)

Brussels 29.9.73. Naturally Magritte and Delvaux turned to surrealism.

\* \* \*

Looking up at her chin and nose from below: alarm at the solid sculptural shape from an unknown quarter.

Grey hair like a handful of iron-filings flung on his head.

Sesquipedalian (given to using long words).

His soft hands reminded me of soap.

The vague awareness of a conscience makes it even more perplexing.

And his shoulders were sloping like a beer bottle.

'The committee recently appointed to review existing legislation on weights and measures went to the root of the matter yesterday and inspected the imperial standard yard . . . It is ordinarily inspected only once every ten years, an occasion which is known as the "decimal comparison of standards".'

And to think that a length of metal, the

standard metre, has also been placed in the Eiffel Tower, as the original 'yardstick'.

R.M.'s grandfather who devoted his life just to 'talking'. He found it easy and enjoyable. He died at 83 in a knife fight.

Shielding her eyes as she entered a room full of people, although it was indoors, at night.

She says 'fantastic' and 'amazing' and I stop listening.

I'd like nothing better than for the sensible pair of tan shoes which have been standing in a tray of water in the window of the traditional menswear shop on Piccadilly, demonstrating their sterling waterproof qualities, to spring a leak or begin rotting, or the tray rust. I always glance when passing, making sure I don't stop.

As she went on speaking, I studied her lips (the flutist).

Unstable landscape. Sands, shifting creekbends, disobedient compasses etc.

When he died, he left him a pair of gates. Story.

*Twelve Footnotes.*

She left him, so he asked a friend to burn relics – her hair, photograph, clothes, letters. The effect in stages on both. Under subject headings?

Unhappy mothers oblivious of sons.

Couples who tour museums, real and imagined.

Rome. Wanting to look at every face passing. Short men with deep dry lines running amok. Details pulled the wrong way, stretched, squashed, bloated. Large fleshy noses. Or pale tight faces with eyes unusually close together. Wealthy women in furs: faces guttered with wrinkles, the large roman nose, layers of powder, bold lipstick. Men of smiling ugliness stepping out from corners or doorways with suede coats, colour slides or maps for sale.

And the city itself has its past exposed like old teeth.

The Tiber looks like an ancient river, but then so do all slow rivers.

In the Flea Market (for sale): ribbons without their medals, country chests, plates from China, horns from animals, car horns, old bras, old brass, seized-up typewriters, metal insects, secondhand nail-files.

The ceiling and end wall (Sistine Chapel) show what a single man has in his power to achieve.

The Vatican. The grandeur of the centre, a kind of hollowness.

Museum for the Struggle of Liberty. Ordinary apartment block (on a street called Tasso). During the occupation the SS bricked up the windows and put in tiny grilles above the height of a man, making about 15 cells on three floors for the interrogation of anti-fascists, killing many. Their photos and blood-stained shirts are displayed in glass cabinets. In some cells, the walls have been covered in glass, preserving the graffiti, blood stains and fingermarks of prisoners. Mostly Italian, some Greek, a little English: JESUS, R.I.P., MY POSITION HERE IS UNTENABLE.

Anonymous courage made more powerful by the startling shabbiness.

A nativity display constructed on the platform by railway workers has men and women gazing at it and throwing money. The whole thing made from blackened railway sleepers and plates.

Even in winter, Rome has the dusty appearance of a hot city.

The necessity to believe in something; literally became a driving force. The Catacombs.

Guide: 'Do you all speak English?'
Australian, loudly: 'Can you manage Australian?'
A form of pride.

The travelling performer had a black Ethiopian wife, four children, three Alsatian dogs. Loud rough voice, dirty hands. While his wife collected the money he sent the dogs through the burning hoops. Things went wrong. The papers torn from an old telephone book wouldn't light. One of the dogs went off for a drink at the fountain. The hoop became too hot to hold. People began to laugh. A man dressed as Father Christmas looked on in the crowd.

Life with such a travelling man (the woman).

　　　　　　　　　·

Romans allow intimate inspection of each other and touching, with arm, hand and finger movements, just as their washing is displayed from their balconies. Similarly, they don't mind being seen eating a visually undignified dish: spaghetti.

Kangaroos often appear in the pages of European novels (Tournier, Lautréamont, Jarry, Beckett, Nabokov etc.) even though – or especially when – the writers have never crossed the Equator.

'Mr Frank and Mr Jack Clatworthy, identical twins aged 20, of Old Cleve Farm, Washford, Somerset, were in adjoining beds yesterday after being injured within an hour of each other in separate accidents in their cars a few miles apart on the same stretch of road outside Taunton.

'They were returning from an hotel staff party when one car overturned and the other went into a hedge. They knew nothing of the coincidence until they awoke in hospital the next morning.'


Story. The thoughts of a woman being painted as Ophelia, lying in a bath.


'Twenty injured in explosion in soda syphon factory.'
I then read every word, looking for small pieces.


F.Mc. always began a hissing sound before laughing, like a hose slithering across cement. It works: I begin nodding and smiling, anticipating his real laughter.


'Yes,' I said, not hearing a word she said.

At Christie's yesterday:
The sale also included a small box of Queen Victoria's wedding cake. The box, neat white cardboard bearing the legend 'The Queen's Bridal Cake, Buckingham Palace Feby. 10 1840', was convincing, but it required faith to recognise the small lumps of brown rock inside as cake. The price was £70 and the purchaser,

Mr Keith Casey, an Australian, was bidding on behalf of a Tasmanian private collector.

'. . . then suddenly the speech gathered momentum. I was caught. I was listening . . . I felt alternatively hot and cold. I didn't know what was happening. It was as though guns were thundering . . . I was beside myself. I was shouting "Hurrah!" Nobody seemed surprised. The man up there looked at me for one moment. His blue eyes met mine like flame. This was a command. At that moment I was reborn.'
– Goebbels encountering A.H. for the first time, 1922.

Fibonacci number sequence: 1,1,2,3,5,8,13,21,34 etc. appears in botany, in spirals (in the curve of elephant tusks, horns of wild sheep and canary claws). The ratio between any two adjacent Fibonacci numbers after 3 is about 1:1.6 – the Golden Ratio.

A turbulent canal.

'When you're in Baltimore, come and see us. The name's Faust. You'll find it in the phone book.'

Misery, sometimes guilt, transferred by a weeping woman to the other person, a man, is counterbalanced by 'nature': the face distorted and reddening into something else hidden, almost abstract. Absorption in such transformation reduces the guilt.

Brief equilibrium.

Preacher (leaning over the pulpit): 'The important time is not in here, but when you go outside – when you return to all those confusions . . .'

V. complains in front of others of his behaviour, as though they never discuss their differences.

Taxi driver in N.Y. who told me he saw a woman being held at knife-point but wouldn't stop because he'd been in jail for a month helping another woman. She was blind and couldn't identify him; and he couldn't prove his innocence.

When I think about myself, I notice I'm frowning.

A cement dog.

Obituary:

Sir Harry Ralph Ricardo, an engineer who made notable contributions to the theory and design of the internal combustion engine, died on Saturday, at the age of 89 . . .

He was described as 'the high priest of the internal-combustion engine'. Etc.

(Thick book with green cover, *The High-Speed Internal Combustion Engine*: its impressive thickness, beautiful cross-section drawings.) The streets of Adelaide.

So the root meaning of 'Ou', the word used to transliterate 'Europe' into Chinese since the sixteenth century, is 'vomit'.

Doctor to woman after hysterectomy: 'We've taken out the school but left the playground.'

How in some faces, men's especially, you can see how they looked when they were about twelve years old; in others you cannot; how some women look like their mothers, even though you may never have met their mothers; and how with some people, men especially, you can see in their faces how their children would look.

'Ever since whenever it was – you know.'

A German officer remarked how strange it was that looting soldiers destroyed musical instruments first – and left almost all mirrors intact. (Junger, in his war-time diaries of the occupation of Paris.)

Girl explaining to downcast friend (attractive blonde) in Indian restaurant: 'He only loves me, because you love me.'

At Highgate cemetery the keeper said he was an ex-champion swimmer. Every day, he said, he swam at the baths, keeping fit, although he was clearly filthy, hadn't touched water for weeks.

'I don't know, what is it you want to see the communist [Marx] for? Everyone comes to see him.'

'Who else is there?'

'I have people here who have had far more influence.'

He led the way to an overgrown grave: MEYER. It was the father of the founder of MGM, film producer to millions.

With his experience of communists, the keeper said he'd never vote for them. 'They can't handle economics. Parties of them come

here holding their hats in their hands. They're
the easiest "touch".'

After pointing to Marx's grave he'd hold his
hand out, and keep holding it out, until they'd
found more money.

'That's no way to run a country,' he said.

Sunday morning. Distraught woman in the
crescent: short dark hair, brown cardigan, arms
folded, gaunt. Walking around it, she kept
bursting out words to herself, shaking her head.
One man crossed to the other side. People leaned
out of windows. M. walked with her for a while,
but the woman kept shaking her head, shouting
out unfinished sentences.

A snake that bites only certain kinds of people.
Those with important theories?

'There has perhaps been a mistake – but of no
great importance – made in the denomination of
this picture.'

Absurd feeling of awkwardness, standing among
other people in lifts.

A nose on her face like an elbow. Pale.

Paris. The barge slowly passing on the Seine had a little girl on a swing on its low roof, the swing making short repeated movements at right angles to the dark length of the barge.

When M. stepped back from the gutter (near les Halles) after almost being hit by a car, she looked up, and although in the midst of recovering balance, instantly smiled: I felt a great stain of affection and respect.

Just going through the motions and producing good taste (the attenuated descendants of the School of Paris).

Seated together in the bar two enormous twins, with the same round face, identical glasses, grey jackets and cardigans underneath. One had fallen asleep. The other took no notice.

Even the garish scraps from his studio are enshrined in the Monet museum. The 'obvious-ness' in the attempt at art leads to a theory or definition. Art 'corrects' nature by an act of translation. Art is imperfect – a human attempt –

unlike nature which is remotely 'perfect'. Painting the lilies, Monet reproduces them his way – converts them into something flawed, faintly within our grasp. His lilies are imperfect. We recognise the attempt: which is largely the power of art.

Weeds in the shallow river trail and drift with faint regularity; and a moth caught on the surface vibrates its wings, creating tiny ripples, drifting to its destruction. (Combray.)

D.G.'s powerful instinct for assembling lists: of things, anecdotes, place-names, interesting locations, and aesthetic impressions.

Arakawa's ambitious subject: *Portrait of a Thought that By-passes Everything.*

Tombs like out-houses, and headstones in the grip of ivy like death itself. A miniature city with small avenues and cross-streets, flowers placed in the front of small 'gardens'. The reduction of scale gives an illusion of temporary superiority to the living walking above the dead. Near the Vorticist tomb of Wilde a party of holocaust survivors chatting by the monuments to the unlucky victims, faces and shadows dappled by the soft shadows of the leaves.

This receptivity for substance ('history' etc.) is becoming too layered. It was always somewhat deliberate, too expectant, anyway.

Two rainbows in the English channel. Pale rain.

On the dole. Every Tuesday I walk to the office and queue in the smoke-filled room at 9am for my cheque. I enjoy the walk. If it's cold I feel warm. A defeated untidiness among the waiting men; but before long I also begin arriving with long hair, unshaven, not wanting to stand out.

Scabs on his face: I thought they were flies.

Story. Take an icon and 'correct' it. Mistake found in a painting, its title, and what is depicted, e.g. *American Gothic*. Figures in it are discovered to be people he knows etc. It can now be revealed. All about them, his plight. A correction. *Bailed Up*?

Suddenly, no birds and I begin to look around.

Story which reproduces painting (*D. Wife*).

Whenever I see an impressive bridge (Bristol), I think of another one.

'Not to descend into chaos, at least not to stay there! But to raise to the light out of chaos, which is fullness, whatever is able and ready to win form. Not to brood! Work! Define, eliminate, give form and completeness.'          – T. Mann

Nasser's story about the man released after many years in jail who killed on his first day out the man he was supposed to have murdered.

Watching the man playing the saxophone on the footpath, he rested one hand on his hip. To show he was listening.

More tact.

Apparently there's a photo of 'The Original Tree of Knowledge'. Somewhere in Baghdad.

Middle-aged man in the dole queue began crying when he reached the counter. Young man in front of me turned and grinned, tapping his head.

Bookseller who 'specializes in Methodism and Mountaineering'.

The drawer of maps (strange profession). Tracing other people's deeds and quarrels, and so on.

Approaching Leningrad: grey with occasional lines barely distinguishable from the scratched aluminium of the plane.

'Any books or newspapers?' Perverse compliment to literature. At *Dead Souls* she nodded solemnly; but at Trotsky seated beside Stalin in *The Russian Revolution* (Moorhead) she beckoned to a man in uniform. He took me into a room and began flicking through it.

His arbitrary method. He'd read a sentence at random, turn some pages, read another sentence, then look again at the forbidden photograph.

Finally he handed it back, stone-faced. And because I had remained silent I stared sourly and remained shaking my head in front of him.

Gradual adjustments of the group: seating positions and how some latch onto others, while one or two are gradually shifted, or sifted to the fringes.

Couple from Hampstead. They brought their own rug to keep warm. Professor of Russian Languages from St Andrews: solitary and bald. Large-nosed spinster fussing with expensive camera who asked loud questions whenever there was a lull. Her curly-haired friend with flat chest and bad skin. Doctor from Brazil with smiling wife; his combed hair. Two young American drama students: the fat one always says 'Gesundheit' when the other one sneezed. Retired professor from Glasgow with French wife noticeably younger. Chinless man with thinning hair in caramel duffel-coat whose wife had recently left him ('So I thought I'd go to the Soviet Union.' Next day. 'Living here couldn't be worse than the living hell I've been through lately.')

Lumps of ice flowing in the rivers like industrial waste, dark figures walking across the frozen canals. Queues for ice-creams on street. Frozen condoms – bloated toadfish – floating in the river outside the hotel. Water jutting out from drainpipes, frozen in mid-air. And the floors of the parks all ice, grey and streaked, like flooded rivers. Not a green leaf anywhere. Mud – everywhere.

A casual lavishness with space.

Conspicuous amount of arm-holding: mainly wives with hand on husbands' arm, but men holding men's arms too. As if they are still recovering from something.

Old buildings painted green, blue or pink, an antidote to the dull weather.

Cold crawling across the face and hands like swarming insects.

The English cramped passion for crosswords, Russia's for the sweeping movement on the chessboard.

People here seem tired. Many more women travelling on trains during the day.

Vodka now resembles melted ice. And its transparency implies space, while the clouded beer of England obeys the island's confines.

As usual I introduce my personality to strangers by harshly overstating everything. Later, a form of disgust with myself.

Intricate oil patterns on the soups (spinach, cabbages, borscht) take me straight back to the greasy patterns in Gogol, Checkov, Dostoevsky.

Museum of Atheism. A bible open to show it had been cut to smuggle a pistol. Photo of Italy's 'weeping mosaic' with diagram showing water tank and pipes leading to Madonna's eyes. Two pulpits, but sermons being 'spoken' were texts from Marx and Lenin.

Museum of Curiosities. Cabinets of costumes from strange lands. Wigwams re-erected etc. Then in a hexagonal room, jars of dead babies on shelves: monsters, Siamese twins, tiny curling foetuses, babies joined at the head, some shape-less like chewing gum, others normal but without arms and legs, one without a nose, one with four eyes and two noses, some without any facial features, or blurred like miniature yellow Francis Bacons.

In the same room the skeleton of a twin-headed goat, its four spare legs swinging in mid-air.


The attendants in the Literature Museum (manuscripts of Tolstoy, Turgenev etc.) seemed to possess the gentleness of Readers.


Moscow. Some people here with heads as red as a copper samovar, and chewing apples.


Queuing for one and a half hours in snow outside Lenin's tomb increases the expectation, as if being kept waiting for an important audience. Glimpse of forests in the speckled green eyes of the guard body-searching for weapons and cameras.

The aura of sanctity radiating from a motion-less figure lying in a three-piece suit and spotted necktie is heightened by the echoing flagstones and the distinct feeling of being underground among the dead where nobody speaks – all part

of the audio-visual display of Lenin's reputa-
tion. A woman in front, from a village by the
look, stumbled when she saw him and began
sobbing. She was led away to lean against the
wall, the guards calling out to her husband shuf-
fling on unaware.

The worship of Lenin is hardly different to
the mass hysteria generated by the British
monarchy or the 'love' of Americans for their
presidents. Outside in the open air my troubled
resentment of crowd behaviour took the form of
wanting to brush rudely against other, probably
decent, pedestrians.


Splayed arms of stubborn fat man, like those
implements for opening lids of bottles and jars.


Tolstoy's grave. Among the birch trees an
unmarked mound which suggested the size of
Tolstoy's stomach. Thin snow, thin trees, thin
wind – strangely thin feelings.

Broken by two sonic booms from jets.


A farmworker passed in a horse and sleigh
loaded with sticks, the sleigh dragging along in
the mud.

All these scratches, scars and soft areas (mud) in this part of the earth.

* * *

Tiredness in the afternoons. I feel like slapping my face.

The problem of seeing certain people. To be forced to listen:

P.H., head bowed, a mixture of Australian no-bullshit and humility;

'I think philosophy is crap.'

'You what?'

'You mightn't think so. I'm just telling what I think. It's *my* opinion.'

Etc.

Story. 'The Kondratieff Wave'. Surf at a place called 'Manly' matches the economic disaster of economic wave. Drowning of a clerk? Wiped out. Interject with statistics. A rhythmic feeling, unfortunately.

Story. 'Catastrophe Theory'. A mathematical model where emotions are measured laterally. (Analytical commentary on an impending action, one thing leading to another.) Measuring fear and rage, hunger and tiredness etc. Measure in inches – ears back, mouth open. Love, lust. Measure? Divergent behaviour.

For some reason I often think of poor old King Farouk.

When she began saying something seriously her voice went deep, almost husky. And I wondered whether she noticed.

Draining vague nausea. Vomiting (the extreme discomfort of an unnatural occurrence).

'. . . his moral inclinations undeveloped: he could do nothing else, otherwise everything would turn out badly; to be a thoroughly moral person demanded complete self-sacrifice.'
– Wagner, his diary

Young woman walking towards me. She is attractive, but has a crippled leg. This in turn pulls down one side of her mouth as she walks. The permanent crease is established (by remote action).

Dog's life. Annoyance of Dogs. A man at work constantly interrupted by distant dogs barking.

Sir Martin Ryle's first important achievement in radio astronomy was to invent a new type of telescope that was equivalent to an instrument with a diameter almost as big as the Earth.

Debating in a performance with J. Beuys among the blackboards (ICA), as he kept writing on them, I felt disadvantaged by the force of his appearance: scarred stretched face, sunken eyes, emphasised by his trademark hat, energised by his waistcoat. He had a kind of relentless courtesy; a kind of earnest discourtesy. He's only doing his job, I thought.

Woman's face: one of those with her mouth fitted upside down.

Pragmatism of women. Often without warning, it appears the dominant characteristic.

'It is, I suppose, impossible to estimate the number of people who, in this age of increased leisure opportunities, have discovered the fascination of tracing their family history, but clearly the number is increasing at an astonishing rate. I know of no other intellectual pursuit which engenders such enthusiasm, which so easily gives a sense of pride in achievement, and which makes one so long to communicate to others and share one's triumphs . . .'

– Fred C. Markwell in *Genealogist's Magazine*

Return to routine.

I think he (my father) sometimes strove for sentimentality, or rather, over-allowed it, which allowed him not to examine his own feelings.

*Wills and Where to Find Them* (J.S.W. Gibson). Also the author of *Wills and their Whereabouts*.

With this weakness, I begin to feel the cold.

Story. Man who collects *sand*. Has more than 400 types. Bondi and Blackpool. Simpson Desert and the rare north-west corner of the Kalahari. He compares the colours and textures, runs the grains through his hand: lemon tones from the Canary Islands, dark stuff from the Black Sea.

Sand grain: infinity. Collector of infinity. Sleep sand – from various eyes?

Slow spread of illness, weakening of the senses, as if the body itself was blurred. It makes me want to talk again – about anything.

His brown hair flattened and tapered after washing like a bandicoot run over on a country road.

Germany Oct. 74. Not so much a country as a vast base to which are bolted and fastened factories and pipelines, and other elaborate protuberances, laced over with bridges and wires, and coated with strips of concrete *Autobahns*; largely a base from which an economy grows.

Even mist swirling among the trunks in the pine forests is at first assumed to be smoke.

Unlike in neighbouring France, no war memorials in villages and towns. Its old teeth have been removed.

Conspicuous number of shops catering to philately. German attempt to rejoin the rest of the world?

Driving through an autumn forest, rust-orange curved away on either side, as if entering the parting of a man's ginger hair.

Unnecessary cultural irritation at the way minor cultural habits form. Middle-aged women in Germany wearing alpine hats and keeping them on in restaurants, men and women in France who follow each other talking with cigarette dangling from one corner of their mouths, Italian men sitting with coats placed over their shoulders. And so on.

Cologne and talkative verger. I stared at him, wondering why.

Crippled hunchback dark against the sky at night (the squat cathedral).

Hotel foyer filled with metallic junk — armour, antique coffee-grinders — chained together to prevent theft.

Rain splattering against the windows of a strange town. As always it makes me think of home, wherever that is.

Puce. Bruised ankles, puce coloured lips and a hat askew.

Living together unmarried, they briefly stayed with P.'s aunt. She went to the lavatory whenever S. used it, and sprayed it – cleansing it of a 'kept woman'.

Englishman said he had just arrived in Australia and driving across the Nullarbor stopped at a small pub in western South Australia and went down to the lavatory outside.

'What are you doing there? Can't you see we're closed?'

'I just want to use your lavatory.'

'Can't you see we're closed,' the pub owner shouted. 'Take your shit somewhere else.'

A mild face. Is that possible?

Necessity of secrets.

'I married him for his mouth. As soon as I saw it, I thought . . .'

For some reason I enjoy seeing other people entering the foyers of hotels.

Hatred of something as ordinary as toast. To explain to anyone would be insufficient.

'He did not know how to curb himself, and so his life, like his poetry, proved ineffectual.'

– Goethe

'But what especially riveted me to him was the utter disinterestedness which glowed in (Spinoza's) every sentence. That wonderful sentiment, "He who truly loves God must not desire God to love him in return," together with all preliminary propositions on which it rests, and all the consequences that follow from it, filled my whole mind. To be disinterested in everything, but most of all in love and friendship, was my highest desire, my maxim, and my practice, so that that subsequent daring saying of mine, "If I love thee what is that to thee?" was spoken straight from the heart.'

– Goethe

Some people I hardly know at all. My brothers, sister.

R.'s secretary was at a weekend party in a grand house. On the Sunday afternoon she went into the drawing room for tea. The hostess was sitting on the sofa, smoking a cigarette, the children playing at her feet. Next to her sat her husband. He was at a queer angle. She then saw a bread-knife in his back. He died on the way to hospital, aged 38, of 'great refinement and wealth', killed by his wife.

Hammersmith Hospital. Nausea and weakness, but unable to block out the words of the incredibly loud doctor and his patient behind the curtain.

'Do you bring up any phlegm in the morning?'

'Yes.'

'How much?'

'Oh, er –'

'A cupful?'

'–'

'An eggcup-full? A teaspoonful? A thimble-ful?'

'Yes.'

A thin 21-year-old who took a drug overdose, his bed fitted with rails. His hair down to his shoulders and vague silly eyes. He has a wandering stupidity, and yet even the old working men include him in their talk and company. On the first visit his father stared at him with bitter contempt, while his mother fussed and tried to be nice. When they left, he said to me, 'She's going to start bawling when she gets home.'

From Barbados, a handsome, once-strong man called Johnson.

'Why did it have to happen to me? It's a hard life. I really enjoyed life. Have two fine boys. I did nothing wrong. Now everything has gone to pieces. My wife, she is a good woman. You should see my wife! A really good woman. I feel sorry for her now. Man! We were saving money. And this had to happen. We were going to build a little house, you know, on the beach back home. My uncle, I've got two uncles, and both have big fishing boats. We'd go out all night. Everyone's got something to eat in Barbados. (Lists all the fish, often their colours.) I had all sorts of jobs. We were saving fine. You know, I wanted to give the boys a good education, and build a fine house – and this had to happen. I really feel bad about that, you've no idea.'

Kidneys had gone: into the machine in two weeks.

Man in pyjamas introduced himself in the first
hour. Shouted, 'Jim. Sorry I can't talk. I'm a bit
hard of hearing.'

Later, being X-rayed together: 'I was a bit
worried about the rent for the council flat.
Instead of letting it worry me I paid in advance.
Three weeks of it. You never know if you'll come
out of these places. You come in, but not always
out.'

Something is bleeding in his throat, non-stop,
and they don't know what.

Thinness of pyjamas when facing someone in
normal dress. Scatty young doctor apologised for
being late (the traffic); and I imagined her
rushing out of the front door, her hair flying.

Swallowing a metal lozenge and several feet
of nylon cord and lying beneath a mass of heavy
black machinery as it tilted over me. Irritation at
the technician's false words of comfort. 'Lovely.
Super. No-one's done it this well. You've really
done it well. You've done it well. If you must
vomit, there's a tray by the side.'

Giardia Lambia.

The feeling, after several days, in hospital that
certain character traits become more established.

Strange greyness beneath the brown of small, large-nosed Indian across the aisle, after his wife and children left. As he stared, he appeared to be trying to speak and slid at an angle from the lunch trolley across his waist. Several beds away the nurse suddenly ran and leapt over him, plates, food and utensils clattering to the floor, and began violently banging his chest. Everybody else stopped eating. She had no time to draw the curtains.

Contrast between the violent noise and movements of human effort and the something-else which is returning almost inexorably to silence and stillness.

Man in next bed (to change the subject): 'I'll say this, they do a very good custard here. And normally I'm not partial to custards.'

'My life then was like a vast newspaper, in which the upper section dealt with the present, the day and its daily reports and debate, while in the lower section the poetic past manifested itself fantastically in continuous nightly dreams like a succession of *roman-feuilletons.*' – Heine

Patient to preacher, doing his rounds: 'You've got a good job, drinking tea all day.'

Facing the preacher, an old West Indian with a trimmed white beard, blind and virtually voiceless – could only slur and mumble – after a stroke, began sliding out of his wheelchair.

'Coffee?' I shouted.

'Wannnnnn.'

'Tea?'

'Wannnnnn.'

'Horlicks? You want Horlicks?'

'Wannnn –' I began forcing Horlicks down his mouth. It kept dribbling. He wasn't swallowing.

'Wannnnn . . . ,' he tried to tell me between mouthfuls. Then I realised it wasn't a drink he wanted – he wanted the preacher. I pointed.

'You're looking well, George,' shouted the preacher.

He slapped him on the shoulder, and George slid almost right off the chair.

'Wannnn.'

'What's that, George? You want a sacrament, George? All right, George. I'm coming around in the afternoon. I'll catch you then, George.'

'Wannnnnn.'

'You want it now, George? Does he want it now? Oh all right, George.' He looked at his watch. 'Whatever's easy for you.'


Cold in the streets. Even the exhaust fumes feel sharp and clean.

A traveller, while adjusting focus (eyes, camera?), sees in rocks the shape of a face vaguely recognisable. Exploration (one with the landscape).

'The world seen in a face.'

Bricks being stacked on the building site clinked like empty bottles.

*Dictionary of Miracles*. Series of minor 'miracles' recalled, reported or speculated upon, including scientific discoveries and coincidences. Several dozen small stories, in a range of styles. Dialogue only, paragraph from newspaper etc.

Definite feeling of not belonging – definitely.

Cleared his throat like wireless static from the 50s.

Story. Cotton dress lands on man's head in strong wind. It could be from the house on the hill etc. He works out her size and appearance, measuring the dress etc. Speculates on her appearance, beliefs. Eventually will find her (then what?).

Symphony concert ruined by the second bass player's foot breaking the line of the stage.

'. . . the complex fate of being an American.'

– James

'Det. Inspector David Burn, aged 42, described at Durham Crown Court yesterday the incident at the Percy Arms Hotel at Otterburn, Northumberland, in which he was shot three times . . .

'With the hotel manager and Det. Constable Keith Wills, he went to Mr O'Conaill's room in the staff block. The manager knocked on the door, saying it was time to get up for work, and a few seconds later the door began to open slowly.

'He continued: "I pushed the manager out of the way and went quickly into the room. I said: 'Hallo, Sean, CID; we want to speak to you,' quite calmly because I did not know what to expect inside the room."

'"Mr O'Conaill was a couple of feet away, a white face in the darkness. Mr Burn continued: "I heard a bang, quickly followed by a severe pain in my left side. I went straight for him with both arms forward and there was a further bang and I felt a violent blow right in the centre of my chest." He still went forward and got hold of Mr O'Conaill's arms, but there was another bang.

"'I felt my stomach going in towards my spine," he said, "and although I arched my back I found I was lifted off my feet and went down on the floor."'

At these times, the hours and days begin crowding.

'Fourteen sketches representing various scenes of bull-fights, shipwrecks, attacks by robbers, fires, fireworks etc.'                                    – Goya

Sound of her laugh: fowls flapping into the air being chased by a rooster.

Possible complications when a man or a woman jumps from a building in N.Y. but lands on a mobster (?) surrounded by bodyguards: expecting assassination attempt everywhere but from above. Mockery of the job description 'bodyguard'.

'In the actual world only compatible things are brought together, and for that reason, in spite of all variety and apparent confusion, the world still preserves a certain regularity in all its parts.'
                                                    – Goethe


Two or three times I made a slightly exaggerated gesture to assist a woman stumbling or lifting a pram up some steps but never went ahead with it.


Unbearable surname: to be called Now. Mr and Mrs Now.


Leaves of a thin tree brushing my face, Holland Park. Not a scratch at all.


Turner (Royal Academy): massive display of strength through honesty. A practical man.


21.11.74. Green diminishing, squares and rectangles. The plane passes through mist – soft European mist, moisture dribbling down the glass – to blue and clear sky above.

A grey quarto book with hard covers,
rounded corners, 'Made in USA'.

*Sydney*
*September 1988–November 2003*

Sept. 12, 1988. Second floor, a building with lift. The different space and air, quality of light, the various different sounds. In the street below light trucks pulling up, roller doors going up. Oriental Enterprises opposite: 'Paging Mr Campbell. Telephone. Mr Campbell.' Desolate after dark and at weekends: blocks of shadows, blank buildings.

The sea-wash of traffic along Broadway, police sirens. The Grace Bros clock chimes on the hour – helped by loudspeakers.

All part of dislocation: the difficulty of sleep, inability to focus: the 'life' I have left behind. And now the arrangement – the tasteful arrangement – of objects, of this new, 'separate' life.

Man standing in doorway in sun. He had a floral shirt, and an amputated leg.

Premier's Award, Melbourne (Sept 16). It was right that the novel was the main award, the 'premier' award, that it was the final main achievement, as it should be.

Such is her decency she is perplexed. Her unhappiness a solid mass. Sometimes she is sullen, bad-tempered. Otherwise it shows in excessive generosity.

Now he is off to the United States. Someone said he was unhappy, on roller skates. His extreme competitiveness, especially among others at a table. His inability not to dominate. His perpetual words, his eagerness to demonstrate his knowledge and grasp of all subjects – his broadness of knowledge and ideas. He is smart and decent. He can maintain friendships only with weaker people, and women.

Always returning to him, discussing him, an irritant, she made the observation that not having had experience of an intimate 'marriage' to another person he has probably never had a harsh true word spoken against him.

Repetitions are worth studying (in literature).

Stravinsky, after listening to someone else's composition: 'But who needs it?'

A. on his wife's dislike of him: 'All I wish is that she'd talk to me as nicely as when she's talking on the phone to other people.'

When I eat alone I consume like an animal. Making noise, slurping out of saucepans etc. Back to distant origins?

The way she strolls naked appears as a parade of ownership. If not happiness, at least contentedness. Meanwhile, the furtiveness of the male.

According to Kandinsky, yellow 'perturbs' man.

'He was proud of his hatred . . .'

17.1.89. All head and bulging blue eyes. No sense of humour, yet could recognise and tell well a story – always based on a person, an experience, usually slightly extreme. Travelled – geographically, intellectually, aesthetically and, apparently, sexually.

These strange confused feelings when a friend, or even an acquaintance, dies at a faraway distance.

Sullen, drab, wary; because of betrayal.

'There are 329 million cubic miles of seawater, 3.5 per cent of which is solid matter. (Land is a puny 30 mill. cubic miles.) One wave in twenty-three, not one in seven, is twice as big as its fellows; one in 1175 three times as big; and one in 300,000 four times. In February 1933, between Manila and San Diego, the *USS Rumapo* met one of the last: it measured 112 feet from trough to crest.'     – *The Faber Book of the Sea*

'Music is a secret arithmetic of the soul, unknowing of the fact that it is counting.'
– Leibniz

C. telling me I live in a 'literary dream', that my conversation has nothing of the everyday world that is of use to her. It was said in a kind of light superiority, as if she had just then thought of it; if I had protested she would have changed her mind.

Blonde came into the shop to buy a cupboard: heavily made-up, perfumed, high heels. Next morning she returned without make-up and perfume, hair undone, looking calmer, almost natural. Her husband was in bed, she said. 'He's not as motivated as I am.'

'The moderation of happy people . . .'
                                    – Rochefoucauld

A man who collects obituaries – only a paragraph each – to form a pattern, some vast story of interlocking exploits.

After dinner, G. felt ill and lay on the floor. His last words: 'No pain, just confusion.'

Newton's sometime assistant, Humphrey Newton, has left the only recorded instance of Newton laughing, when someone asked him what use it was to study Euclid's *Elements*.

'. . . I behaved as I did later with people I loved too much; I was speechless, motionless, stupid and ungracious, sometimes giving offence through excess of devotion and lack of self.'
                                    – Stendhal (*H. Brulard*)

A *loud* story. Impossible?

Children climbing, swinging and hanging from low heights in the new playground at the bend in the street, as if happily allowed to obey the original four-legged instinct.

Man who polishes the front of his house every morning with a rag.

Woman has her nose altered by surgery, because 'it threw an ugly shadow'.

'I wish I'd never met you.' But then she paused and quickly hugged me.

'It takes years to destroy a person's love; but no life is long enough to lament this murder, nothing is more of a murder.'          – Canetti

Another and then another and yet another land-scape.

Now that she isn't here – in her absence there are some things I would like to ask her.

Parramatta Road. Hearse with coffin and loaded with flowers being pushed at traffic lights by one of the funeral directors, all in black. Giving death a push; or pushing a body towards a ceremony.

For example, a jugful of tears (a glass jug). By a bedside table. Leaking?

Oneirocritic. A judge or interpreter of dreams.

C.B., a purser with P&O for 23 years before marrying T., died on Thursday on a P&O voyage with T., and was buried at sea.

'Like many men, he was rendered wicked by misfortune.'
                                        – Conrad

Girl at mirror arranging her hair severely, twisting it like a mechanic tightening part of an engine. Then turning from the mirror with a relaxed expression.

'I'm retiring two years early. I've thought about it a lot, I gave it a lot of thought. But there was

no point ending my life in an unhappy situation. What am I going to do? Good question. At the Blind Institute they have volunteers reading bits from newspapers. I'd like that. And I've been at the women's home at Norwood, playing the organ. It's an old pedal organ, but I like them. The old ladies sit around the organ, some of them are not 100% mentally, but I enjoy it.'
— J.H. on the phone, visiting Sydney

The way she takes what's available — the pedestrian button at lights, the teller machine in banks — is that of a *daughter*.

His attitudes all opened at once like a fan — or a hand of cards.

'Here we go, here we go, here we go' — Irishman at the table, beginning to eat.

Fat woman in a swimming pool: banging her arms onto the water and grimacing like a wrestler pinned to the mat.

He looked like a plumber who'd lost his tools.

T.'s wife on the footpath. Because she was pale and plain, I noticed for the first time her unusually speckled brown eyes. Otherwise she looks like a mother.

'I love the rule that corrects the emotion.'

– Braque

Bruxism – teeth-grinding.

As she watched a woman on the street holding a baby up to her face saliva filled her mouth.

Lying on the floor on an elbow on a cushion gazing at the fire, and gradually becoming drowsy at the lack of oxygen.

Short grey hair, clear skin, strong teeth exposed to the air by much spontaneous smiling – her smiling, a form of language. 'I know this *wonderful* prostitute in Sydney. She is a *wonderful* person.'

She clenches herself, and embarks on a rocking motion at the thought.

Albert Ryder's brother in the 1840s, a sailor, was so happy on his return to land that he kissed a pig.

'When that which is said figuratively is taken as though it were literal, it is understood carnally.'
— St. Augustine

*Brisk.* A disappointing word. To use it is to appear 'brisk'.

She smiled: her teeth cracked, disintegrated. The man's smile, more of a wince as if the sun was in his eyes. (Thin man, standing behind the counter.)

March 17, Hume Highway. Soft blurry tones of hills and trees. Gradually a pinkish haze. Rounded caramel hills. A line of trees following a distant fence (up a hill).

The world seen in a face. It would only be a brief part of the world.

A face in the shape of a house, a tall narrow house.

'If he was singing for corned-beef, he wouldn't get the strings.'


The bitter harsh side of her mother overtakes the simple goodness of her father.


Writers who write little are naturally more sensitive to failures.


He knew everything there was to know about poultry.


Six days of rain, day and night. A curtaining of the senses; hours levelling out into sameness, like the evenness of the rain itself, made steadily more even by the general reduction of colours. Vague feeling of claustrophobia indoors – increased or aggravated by the reduced field of vision. Drove to Windsor to see the flooded river. A few people stood at the edge of the water, at the flood's perimeter, simply looking (recording the scene). West of Richmond, six men got out of a van, came forward and began putting a boat into the water, each man moving slowly, methodically, hardly speaking, performing a task, not recreation. Starting the outboard they steered the boat along over the submerged road, and disappeared. It began raining heavily.

She was regal, almost absurdly regal, as they checked each other over.

Near Bathurst. Difficulty of describing sunsets. The casual violence of its sensations, its vastness: as if, in the car, slowly approaching somewhere unearthly, and so the loneliness in the beauty.

Clouds draw attention to themselves. They ask to be described. And it is generally a pleasure to do so.

The enormity and the modesty of clouds.

'Religion is advice.'

Infantile Paralysis. Story. The title produces the story.

Man with arm in plaster in bank said he had fallen off a roof trying to climb into his girl-friend's window. He explained loudly, glancing at other customers.

'Leslie gave me a car but I broke it.' Spoke very slowly, otherwise she'd be 'dizzy'.

With his cheek pressed against the strings, the intensely concentrating cellist appeared to be picking his nose with his fingers, and getting pleasure out of it.

My father's friends: I don't recall any.

'Leave sunsets to the sunsets themselves.'

Nine. As a surname.

Young man and Asian woman in playground, early Sunday morning. She, neat, her jacket over her shoulders. He, playing with their child on the seesaw. So happy is the woman, she is constantly talking. She is talking too much – about 'nothing' – so that although he is with her the man becomes uninterested, more with the child.

The underside of mushrooms imitates charcoal-grey feathers.

Through a window: a baby being passed around among seated figures, the baby above their heads.

West Africa on the map. Timbuktu near the Niger River: wondered at the difficulty of reaching it. Heat and emptiness, the sadness of Africa, as traced on a map. The pleasure at gazing at maps in comfort.

Town called Man in Ivory Coast.

I am not doing anything. Barely even thinking. 16.6.89.

One half of the table slurping and sucking on their bony food, and reaching across others, and tilting plates and shovelling the food in, no-one waiting, while the other end talked and shouted and interjected. I wondered what I was doing there.

And there is something essentially glib about a man who in six days or six months makes a painting of an oak tree that would have taken a hundred years to grow, or rocks that may have taken millions of years to form and wear, merely to produce an impression of the real thing.

Be less enthusiastic; considerate and sober in praise: mature.

This vagueness, it resembles bad weather.

Unnecessary 'knowledge'.

Fat bank teller, shirt sleeves rolled up just above the wrists. Accordingly, his rather dainty counting of money.

Philosophers' lives. Combine their stories. Always wanting to be teachers.

Some of the clothing in the crowd creaked in the dark (at *Die Walküre*).

'I am possessed with a mania for comparisons.'

Corrugated iron church (near Oberon): more like a shearing shed. A brown horse standing against the entrance, out of the wind.

Snow all the way up the trunks of eucalypts: white and grey-white. Snow and cold are always a reminder of the harshness of this isolated planet, and how humans have softened it, to remain living. A smoking chimney in the snow: sign of ordinary decent pleasures.

Pink cockatoo flew alongside the car like a hawk.

Once there were too many books; and now there are too many paintings.

Young woman carrying parcels – it gave her a double-chin.

Father and son: taking it in turns to wear the same hooked nose.

To die and be buried unknown and unmarked in a foreign country. Exaggerates the futility of life.

No difference (Sept 22. 1989).

A daughter with her mother goes up to her father in a hotel foyer and sees in his expression he doesn't want to see them.

'Man with a boy's head' (soldier's description of bank clerk who was incompetent officer in Palestine).

'He had so many things wrong with him it was difficult to know what was right with him.'

In the supermarket the lights suddenly went out and the women erupted with little cries and sighs, as if it was a party game from childhood. Young man ostentatiously continued shopping, using cigarette lighter.

Sparrows like pegs on a line.

Seriously. No-one took him seriously!

The confused-gender laugh of J.M.: began like a motorbike kick-starting.

The actor. He was like a room, a tasteful room where every other day the furniture kept being rearranged.

Honolulu Airport. Two Canadian newlyweds, as happy as large children.

Toronto. Young bearded driver (after fooling around on car phone):

'Have you been to the Great Barrier Reef?' 'Yes.' 'Wow. The longest living organism in the world. I read it only yesterday.'

Niagara. The balustrade has been built alongside the flowing water as close as possible to where the water rushes over the lip, a slippery rush – about an arm's length away – bottle-green lake water, sliding over into translucent skin-coloured. The scene is brought forward in the North American way: the spectator/consumer is given good value, satisfaction.

The Victoria Falls are instead seen across a canyon head-on, at a distance.

H.'s voice, long distant. Small.

*Victoria and Niagara: a comparison.*

Feeling of reduction, incompleteness.

A woman threw her baby over the Falls, but was prevented from following, and is still alive.

New York. Early evening in heavy rain; and illuminated like a vast, leaking engine.

The thirty-eight Velasquezs at the Metropolitan: portraits of adults look directly at the painter who is replaced by the viewer. The children look sideways. Thin paint, unlike Rembrandt. An extreme naturalness; a transparent objectivity. And so the figures come forward from the walls with a natural living force.

Women putting earrings on. Their faces change as they alter themselves.

He missed having a harelip by three minutes.

Dakar 27 Oct., 9.45pm. Thick hot air smelling of shit and rotting vegetation. Pale yellow headlights of traffic. The square with thick trees, dark figures seated on cement benches. The prostitute in denim accosted me as I looked at nothing in a shop window.

Trunks of trees twisted like the limbs of nearby lepers. Tall night-coloured men walking in their flowing jellabas which look like night-gowns, and so they appear in broad daylight to be sleep-walking.

The keen interest women take in human affairs shows in their faces. Here in Africa, and elsewhere.

Bananas more than a foot long: in the shape of Islam.

'The telephone is broken.'

Baobab trees, jacarandas, a single eucalypt.

Goree. Enormous rusting guns on top of this island, hanging down and pointing like hopeful penises.

Mass on Sunday: so many twittering sparrows inside the church it was difficult to make out a word the priest said.

Men playing cards on a blanket.

Mauritania, the last country in the world to abolish slavery (in 1980). The size of Belgium and until recently not a single building of two storeys.

More soldiers than police.

Bamako, Mali. Pink-brown dust – on ledges of buildings, on cars, on the leaves of palm trees, shoes and clothing. Man kneeling to peer under broken-down car, as if praying to Mecca. Leper crawling along the ground, raising his head like an angry lizard. His angry eyes fixed on me. A simpleton came out from the shadows and grabbed my hand. Albino twins seated on either side of their mother in the gutter, their pale faces spotted with scabs. And at intervals the erect beauty of the women, their bright clothing and turbans as optimistic plumage.

Man pushing wheelbarrow containing sewing machine.

A man with birdcage on his head, the tiny red and orange birds fluttering about.

Dwarf in a floral suit.

Tarts in bar, twisting around on stools.

Folksinger: he sang a folktale from a Bamaro village. A man kept hunting an animal that was really a beautiful woman. He used all his skills to hunt it/her. The young men in the village, they asked him how he did it, how did he become so skilful. His wife became jealous. He killed the beautiful woman and she turned back into game. The wife was going to cook her.

Impressive conference centre, with dust on floor.

Slight feeling of dislocation walking through W. Africa. There are no cultural references, no literary reminders. The blue flowers alongside a river in Georgia, mentioned by Turgenev.

Beggars with the most dreadful politeness.

Universal power of the smile: when offered, it is invariably returned, larger.

Gratitude of some sort of contact.

Camel coloured desert with unexpected congestion like a scab (Timbuktu).

Loose sloping sand, building up against the bushes, poles, walls: the Sahara creeping south. The walls themselves are the same colour as the sand. Men with blue turbans wrapped around faces, just the eyes showing.

Extremely handsome men, hard-looking men. Women here don't cover their faces, but often their mouths with a corner of their shawl (*afar*) when they pass a man.

Sand in ears, hair and eyes; it's ankle deep in the houses and the mosque; sand in the food, the wholewheat bread especially. Violent heat; the hot sand. The Sahara outside the town: an immensity of pale dunes, swept clean and shaped by the wind, dizzy circular patterns repeating. All smooth, clean, not a speck of rubbish. Late afternoon, solitary Arabs walk out into the dunes and sit cross-legged on top of one or throw themselves down on the sand like children.

Desert at the end of every street.

Tiny birds dusted a pale pinkish-red, like hot coals – the Senegal Fire Finch.

Blind man led about by a boy; hand on the boy's shoulder has worn a hole in the shirt.

Rarely a man seen walking with a woman. Men sitting on sand in groups. Talking among themselves women nevertheless sound as if they are loudly arguing.

Several years ago this man broke his leg and got gangrene; now with one leg, he makes musical instruments. A missionary gave him an aluminium crutch, just one. His curious hunted expression makes him look dangerous.

Young Tuareg in blue. His brothers seated, Hammoden 25, Hallah 17, Lamin 23.

'Place of 333 saints' – sign in town.

Mopti. Heat and the 'heaviness' of the African people, men and women each trying to make some sort of living. Takes the form of constant slowness. Here the swamp, the slow river, the large birds (hawks?) floating overhead.

'My home is not your home!'

The waiter was smelling the glasses. He had his nose in them. Seeing me, he remained expressionless.

Djenne. The large mud mosque: 'in the ramparts of Djenne a young girl, sacrificed of her own volition . . . was buried alive to ensure the prosperity of the market.'

Arab men shaking my hand, then touching their hearts in the traditional way.

Vagueness gazing at the mud houses and the large mud mosque. These unhurried people all remote from me – many stages removed. And so in the heat I felt a certain indifference.

Mopti–Bamako, 625k – nine and a half hours. Windows and doors of the Peugeot 'bush taxi' remained shut in the heat. Ten people including the driver, mostly broad-beamed women with henna-painted hands and feet, one with a baby who had dysentery, crying. Another woman had only one eye. The man next to me wanted my watch. Two goats in hessian bags tied onto the mound of luggage on the roof. After a few hours a kind of numbing sensation which prompts a hazy introspection. As monotonous scenery passed I again dwelt on unhappiness I have caused – as well as happiness.

Six checkpoints. At the first, two soldiers looking in pulled me out, asked for money. Naturally the other passengers were irritable with me for the delay.

Skin began peeling from the tips of my fingers – diet, or something I had picked up from the many different hands I had touched – but within days of leaving Timbuktu they returned to normal.

To write a novel which has the firm interest of a biography; more powerful than everyday life. The 'realism' of a biography is more firmly based, even though it has few of the novel's advantages.

There were trees with trunks that looked like iron ore.

Early morning. Before long the earth would begin steaming.

Smiled, as if rain was hitting him on the face.

Even a woman's waist is funnel-shaped to be poured into; while the male's waist is roughly straight and parallel.

Red bricks of the house the colour of lamb chops, which gradually turn brown in the heat.

Simple statement of a missing third finger (man on a building site).

Breasts that were of more interest to her than others.

The shoemaker and his medieval movements. Including the leathery gloom of his shop.

Women together make each other feel and behave more like women.

Even in Australia – the millions of manufactured rings, worn on the fingers of women.


Colin McCahon visiting L.B. in Melbourne 1951 was the only painter she really didn't take to, 'as a person'.


'This morning I was bled . . . I have great hopes of recovery. Nevertheless I want to say farewell to you, in case this letter may be the *ultima*. I truly love you, and you are not one of a crowd.

Farewell, take events cheerfully as they come.'

– Stendhal's last letter to his friend Di Fiore.


Earlier Stendhal had written, 'There is nothing ridiculous about dying in the street, provided one does not do it on purpose.'


'Common as rain . . .'


The moist lips of men with beards.


Accidental clarity.

Refugees and the woollen scarf.

Bare hills like crumpled bed sheets (outside Auckland). Elsewhere fire tracks cut like waterfalls.

'It was . . . ungodly, unusual. I hated it.' Train driver in NZ recounting earthquake while on bridge.

Thinning ginger hair, long face, moist lips. His perpetual nervousness. He lives in architect-designed units combined into one for the use of his ancient aunt. She leaned over the balcony, 'Three men have come in . . .' He took two sleeping pills before we arrived, to calm himself, he said. Many bottles and jars beside his bed, the mattress on the floor. 'Thank you, thank you . . .' he repeated. Talking rapidly, brokenly, distractedly. 'Money is truth,' he said several times, closing his eyes, almost rocking in his seat. He had virtually lost the family fortune. As he spoke honey slowly fell from the spoon onto his trousers. A long black painting behind the piano: had to crawl to see it. Upstairs where his aunt lay in bed, he showed without a word another painting.

'Thank you, thank you, thank you . . .' he

said as we left. Such a collapse of a man does make one wonder about his childhood. Auckland.

A jar full of wedding rings at pawnshop, woman making a selection: 'No, I want sixteen carats!'

Two children found a man's body in gully and for more than a year kept going back to look at it as it decomposed, without telling anyone.

'He had a pathological hatred of – what was it? – butter.'

Said he didn't believe in Christianity but 'Godianity'.

While thinking about some distant place, he also saw where he was standing.

Continuously twisted or broke her ankles.

'. . . naïve, whining and market-place romanticism'.        – Julia Kristeva, on feminist fiction.

Quite often 'love' stops dead or drifts off.

If dreams were unnecessary, natural selection would have removed them by now.

Story called Sunday or Monday. (What then?)

'Hate is a sadness . . .'                                    – Spinoza

Even when talking normally I often feel an unpleasant, sour expression on my face.

'. . . the tendency to feel contempt (in the end, it is a beginner's emotion).'

Early teens . . . looking up to older men, impressed by and interested in their long experience. And the men too with their larger worn hands and faces spoke, down to me, though matter-of-fact, aware of their position.

Bandsmen leaving in their small cars.

To others I complain about things, yet hardly ever complain to myself.

The only time we felt close that weekend was when we squatted together on the road scraping up horse manure, one scraping with a piece of cardboard, the other holding the box.

'. . . the sentiment of pity is nearly allied to contempt, which is a species of dislike with a mixture of pride.'                    – Hume

A leisurely journey (story). Wandering over a face (face lying upwards), over each part – cheek, mouth, breath, eyes etc. – the narrator traces story of the person's life. Lips did this . . . which resulted in . . . The eyes saw . . . etc. She overheard . . . etc.

Waiting at the dentist, alongside a 91-year-old deaf man. Born in Tasmania: worked on the railways, in a foundry, cane-cutting. In 1935 he fell from a ladder, broke an arm, a leg and twisted spine. There were two kinds of doctors: company doctors and doctors. 'Company doctors only tell what the bosses want to hear, you see.' He was paid $1035 for the spine, $600 for the leg, $340 for his eyes – 'I've got cataracts from the grinding wheel.' After the 'Hitler war' his daughter, then six, was running across a street in Carlton when a drunk – 'he had a keg rolling about the back of his van' – was saying hello to his mates on the footpath, and swung right across and 'hit my little girl.' Her mouth was all pushed in, her legs were curled up and broken. She died in half an hour. Eleven years later her mother died and was 'buried on top of her'. 'My other daughter lives down Frankston way. No good. The first man who smiled at her she married. He'd stepped off a boat without two bob to rub together.' He spoke in detail of mechanical things – he had the first AJS motorbike in Tasmania. How they worked, how he repaired things. After ninety-one years he could recall a day in Tasmania when the chain on a motorbike broke, out in the country. He made a linkage from wire and rode back to town with it clicking. He gave a laugh for the first time at the recollection. A heavy man with a ruminating pout.

Her mother looked like an angry duck; her father, broader, like a frog.

The ratio between reading and writing: too much reading.

Dunedin 22.7.91. The Presbyterian darkness, not only the hills, the houses. The Professor, a communist, in his tall freezing house with his unhappy wife, the opera singer. His unusual mix of the informal and the slangy. Embarrassed at being a professor?

A piano teacher has planted himself in my mind; I don't even know what he looks like.

Two black cats standing against each other like bookends.

When the crippled woman yawned she looked normal.

The 92-year-old man recently a father demonstrated his virility to the cameraman by chopping wood. His young (38) wife looking on had a mass of buck teeth.

Those rib cages piled in the back of the truck leaving the butcher's looked like cane baskets.

He wanted a life as uneventful as possible, so as to be able to observe. He said while eating at the table. (W.S.)

Only shook his hand once, although they were close friends, and that was the day he told me he was dying.

Biographer robbing from his subject – taking at will – like a handbag snatcher who doesn't even run away.

In African sculpture there is a mask used to remind people of human imperfections.

'My wife and I sat down one night and wrote down every person we knew. We stopped at 390.'

Cuts and scratches take longer to heal; and cuts and grazes leave a scar now.

The tall American (yellow hair) who went and lived in India to catch cobras. 'I guess I just don't like people.' Why 'guess'? *Does* he or not?

'She made necklaces out of lavatory chains. She was very clever.'

He saw bluntness as a virtue, as if bluntness itself was truth. And all the members of the family inherited this bluntness as a virtue and accordingly developed enemies and strong neck muscles.

In 1891, when he was 25, Jawlensky met the daughter of a general, a woman painter four years his elder, Marianne van Werefkin. For the next 30 years she would dominate his existence, as chief muse and intellectual lodestar. She accompanied him to Munich, sacrificing her art for his, and bringing with her her personal maid, the 15-year-old Helene, who would later bear Jawlensky's son Andrew. Meanwhile, Werefkin remained a constant presence, living with the family, even into Andrew's teens . . .

Tendency (Christian name of a woman). Her name was Tendency.

'My poor son,' dying father to son. Humorously, mockingly.

Hume Highway. Unpainted shearing shed floating on its shadow in a paddock, moored to the house by the slack line of the fence.

Camel-coloured rams, their expressions like camels too. Their horns pressing in like commas, squeezing out the expression of haughtiness.

From the moment she got on a subject she was like a snowplough on a train.

*Eucalyptus*, from the Greek: 'well' and 'covered'. Until they open, ready for fertilisation, the eucalyptus buds are covered, in effect putting a lid on the reproductive organs. Perfect.

By Skidelsky's biography, Keynes was an immensely attractive man, at the same time repulsive.

'Money . . . is, above all a subtle device for linking the present to the future.'      – Keynes

An Australian in England was almost killed by a hit-and-run driver. For seven months he lay in a coma, in an obscure hospital, unable to say who he was. To his mother, Polish, in Melbourne, he had disappeared without trace. She decided to sell three Morandi drawings, and to go to England to find him. Then a friend visiting the hospital happened to glance into the ward and recognised him.

'It's all so meaningless we might as well be extraordinary.'  – Nietzsche, quoted by Francis Bacon

How night and sleep break our lives into regular sections. Inconceivable to live a life of uninterrupted daylight – a nightmare.

She cleaned her teeth vigorously, the way she tore open envelopes.

Newspaper headlines pasted on wall of American poet's lavatory:
– Burglars take guillotine and Hitler's piano
– Ex-Pittsburg salesman may rule Brazil
– Seagull causes jockey's death

'The intelligence is defeated as soon as the expression of one's thoughts is preceded, explicitly or implicitly, by the little word "we".'
– Simone Weil

Optometrist. Examined first one retina and then the other with alarming intimacy, her breath audible, nose brushing my cheek, as she slowly circled my eye like a skindiver inspecting coral.

While talking to some people, but not others, I avert my eyes.

On the verandah (Barkly St.): shadow of an airliner crossed the backyard, pointing like an arrow. That it crossed that lawn in the midst of other lawns; that I happened to be standing there; that it was about as large as a man; that it flowed over the back fence. The noise of the plane itself was only faintly heard.

The sand dunes I saw in the Sahara repeating to infinity: they have a name, *ergs*.

Wife coming towards husband waiting in car: using particularly small steps, like a geisha girl.

P.'s step-mother, always complaining about something, even when putting on a blouse: 'Don't you just hate doing up buttons?'

She had six children in South Australia. All died of scarlet fever. Then widowed, she married again; and had five healthy children.

Sydney, 15.10.94. Faint thickness of air, the glittering of windows and distant surfaces. Its enormous sky and curving streets, rising and falling, allow entry. Welcomed me back.

People like to explain the many keys on their rings.

S. lowering her head and lowering her voice, unable to answer ordinary questions.

'It is difficult for a man to speak long of himself without vanity; therefore I shall be short.' Then seven pages follow. Hume, *My Own Life*. The title has a simple 'modesty'.

'As randy as a leather-punch.'

The greatest painters make a tree as elemental as rocks – as if this tree stands for all trees (Courbet's oak, Cézanne's pine, Rembrandt's etching of three).

I had always thought the last word written by Tolstoy in his *Journals* was *me*; aghast, I told others about it; yet when I checked today it was instead: 'Everything is the same; worse even. If only I don't sin. And don't bear malice. I don't at present.'

13.1.95. Lately I have felt myself sliding into a flat, factual mournfulness in speech, in response to her questions. Largely a result of inexplicable embarrassment.

18.1.95. Yet another address (official). All this mobility – Chippendale, North Fitzroy, New York, Rose Bay, and now Elizabeth Bay – a form of evasion.

A 'muddy' smile. Just as there is a foolish smile.

R. arrived from England in the 1950s. At the first estate agent in Kings Cross she asked for a room for that night. After a few days the landlady, who had a German name, asked if a man could inspect the old clock in her room. He was an antique dealer. He arrived, glanced at the clock. Later he was in the kitchen with the landlady drinking beer. They invited her to join them.

When the landlady said she had washing to get off the line, the antique dealer turned to R.: 'We will go to dinner tonight.' She began seeing him regularly. After several years, she said to him, 'I am almost forty. I like being with you, but my family think I should be married. Let me know on Tuesday. Otherwise I'll have to find someone else.'

Tuesday night they went out to dinner. She waited. A few minutes before midnight he took from his pocket a ring. 'We will get married.' For a wedding present he gave a large parcel. It was the clock he had 'inspected' in her room years earlier. Over thirty years they never argued. He died suddenly. A few weeks after his death R. visited the landlady. As she was about to go, the old woman said, 'There is something you should know. He had become very lonely. He asked me, "You must help me. I am going mad. I want to meet a woman." You had just rented your room. We arranged for him to inspect the clock. He was really inspecting you. If he liked the look of you, he would come back in a few days. It worked out very well. You've had a long marriage.'


The cellist is more neurotic. Having to carry the large hollow instrument wherever he goes, whereas the pianist only takes along his hands.

From an early age I could see that women were more attentive, more softly attentive, than men. That's the trouble.


Claude Lanzmann's *Tsahal*, Jewish Film Festival. The former soldiers interviewed – impressive. Recalling 'very difficult' battles they spoke matter-of-factly, level, no quips. They all spoke in a calm serious way. No mock heroics, no casual deliberate modesty, no drollness. Officers, some high-ranking, sat among the soldiers; leaders stood out from the rest, though. 'There is no distance here,' said one, 'but under certain circumstances there would be distance.'

These Israeli men each had a pen clipped to their shirt pocket.

The mostly Jewish audience made this five hour documentary oppressive. They watched and listened intently. Their combined assumptions also made for heaviness. Their breathing, heavy and approving; their laughter.

The elderly man seated next to me. Alert with small steady watery eyes. He'd started Lawrence Dry Cleaners many years ago. The Holocaust would not exterminate the Jews. 'A heavy pruning,' he said to me, 'strengthens the tree.'

Woman visiting daughter in Tasmania: 'I've gone through every room in the house and I haven't found a single photograph of me.'

Eyebrows. Oddly, specifically human. Nothing more.

Wanted to ask young woman in shorts which revealed moles if she was a first born. In the post office.

His description of lack of success in love: 'If it was furniture it would be covered in sheets.'

'Vainglory and curiosity are the twin scourges of our souls.'                                    – Montaigne

Nibbling chocolates, the elderly Greek said eucalypts were grown in front of houses in Alexandria to ward off evil spirits, including diseases.

A strange dislocated mind, unreliably unreliable. (C.)

Early Saturday morning, Rushcutter's Bay. Two young women noticed a man lying facedown, near yacht club. While one stayed back the other tiptoed *on the grass*, and leaned towards the man who was merely sleeping. One way to approach a possible death in the suburbs. And his down-turned arm and hand made a shape like a swan's neck.

At the film *Gettysburg* surrounded by the smell of someone's rotting teeth in the dark. D. noticed too. He thought it was appropriate. Tried breathing through mouth. Then searched around with my tongue to see if it was my own teeth.

'It was not absolute nothingness. It was a kind of fearlessness without any definition.'

– Augustine

Women and wistfulness. An easy effect in art, a curse, and irritating in life. And why?

Tattooists first practise on, and ruin, one of their own legs.

Safety in numbers! Pedantry, stultifying effects of. A muffling through voicing of facts – obviousness stated with real solemnity.

Psychoanalysts: the new priests. They run their fingers all over a person without touching them.
It would take an indignant, curious book to 'place' them in our present civilisation.

A courthouse on the street. Citizens could pause on the footpath and look in through the open window at proceedings.

'How vain painting is, exciting admiration by its resemblance to things which we do not admire in the originals!'                                    – Pascal

A large hypnotic jaw.

He knows what your next sentence is, and so doesn't want to hear it.

Possibly a father's disquiet at a man sleeping with his daughter is the obscure feeling that a part of him is being slept with by the same man.

Kings Cross, mid-afternoon: long-haired man walking methodically across traffic, eyes fixed on small man ahead who was half skipping, taunting. Then he broke a beer bottle and holding it forward began to run after him. The small man stopped and turned and with a single punch knocked him down. The taller man then took off his shirt and bare-chested – a man returning to and revealing the primitive – ran after him again. Once more the small man turned, went into a crouch, and knocked him down. Part-aboriginal, ex-boxer. His companion also small had a worried expression, almost whispering, 'Shayne . . . audience . . . audience.' But he was winning and wasn't listening. He hit the bare-chested man on the nose, and as he rolled on the footpath pushed two fingers into his eyes. Later the tall man went away, face covered in blood, and squatted behind some bushes, like a dog, followed by only one person, a woman.

Man blind from birth (R. McC.) returned my call: dreaming, he said, he sees nothing, all is blank. He dreams only smells and touches.

Prosper Mérimée, a friend of Stendhal's, wore a signet ring inscribed (in Greek): 'Remember to be mistrustful.'

Art criticism: 'A steady iron-hard jet of absolutely total nonsense as if under great pressure from a hose.'                                    – Empson

Woman in doctor's surgery had a collapsible walking stick which she referred to as 'he', as if it was some sort of animal – a man even. She could be quite severe on the walking stick, rebuking it loudly. Generally though she treated the collapsible walking stick kindly enough.

'I try to be . . . loyal to all men' – Pascal. What can he mean? I can be loyal only to a few; how to be loyal to men in general?

R.K. lying back in the pillows the day after his hip replacement, thin, pale and bruised; he looked like a very old Jewish bookseller, almost dead.

Outside King George Hospital for women the white sculpture appears as a woman from behind, a king from the front. In the 1950s(?) a Romanian carved it on the spot, and as he worked nurses from all floors called out and jeered. He moved to Melbourne. Before the war he was commissioned by a wealthy businessman in Romania to sculpt his daughter. They fell for each other. The father tried to stop them. They married and came to Australia. They were poor. She had to work. They had a son. R. visited them in Melbourne. The wife was out working. The son had grown into a young man. The sculptor was asleep, just returned from visiting Europe. Soon afterwards he died.


A deafening cat.


Tolstoy (*Anna Karenin*) never hides behind obscurity, not even poetic obscurity – a literary Velasquez. His transparency can be perilously plain, too like ordinary commonsense. Amongst this 'plainness' he'll toss off an arresting truth, e.g., 'And another thing, women are more materialistic than men. We make something immense out of love, but they are always terre-à-terre.' Many very short chapters. Often these short chapters have an 'unconscious' contrast between pleasure and physical surroundings, broken by confusion over a woman; and – the very next short chapter – the cold triumph of Anna's husband at a committee meeting, followed by his confusion when confronted by his wife and her demands. An emotional zigzag. Tolstoy seems to give equal weight to men and women – rare in any writer.

The repetition of 'house' and 'home' in *A.K.*'s second paragraph never fails to draw me in, and further in – to another world.

Somewhere a man who has never seen a river.

At the front of the farmhouse there was also a huge collection of rusted broken-down machinery. At dusk these appeared as disabled insects.

Paragraphs as paddocks.

His hair cut short revealed a birthmark: his face in permanent shadow.

In the next room a woman talking on the phone: 'My first thoughts were – I didn't think you'd answer.'

Genghis Khan, questioning his Mongol comrades-in-arms about life's finest pleasures and being told it lay in falconry, replied, 'You are mistaken. Man's greatest good fortune is to chase and defeat his enemy, seize his total possessions, leave his married women weeping and wailing, ride his gelding and use the bodies of his women as a nightshirt and support.'

C., eldest of nine children. Her father, Chinese, in Tasmania, didn't marry until he was 35. His father died when he was 15; alone he built up a business, fruit and vegetables. He converted to Catholicism. Tasmania seemed too small to find a good Chinese wife. He asked his priest to look out for one; he had contacts with priests around the world. A priest in the West Indies knew a Chinese man with six unmarried daughters. C.'s father wrote a letter, introducing himself. *Two of them passed the letter along. The third daughter replied.* For two years they wrote letters. The Tasmanian went to the West Indies; they married a few months later. As a father, he was strict, traditional, rhetorical. To the daughters he seemed ridiculous. One morning he read the lesson at church, stepped down and in front of his wife and congregation had a heart attack.

'He would have liked dying like that, in front of an audience.'


He said small dogs always run into the room with tail wagging at the sounds of their arguments or lovemaking.


Shaking George Foreman's hand – it was hardly an ordinary hand. And he'd stepped forward with it out-stretched. 'Good on you, George.' Foreman: 'Even-ing, friend.' A puffy soft hand. His bodyguards were black and wore black shirts, black suits, white shoes. The gold jewellery favoured by old prize-fighters standing around nearby.

The Russian psychoanalyst in the 1930s who had a portrait of Pavlov on the wall at day, Freud at night.

Indignant. Too often indignant.

Large white cockatoo in one of the trees at the Scottish Hospital was being attacked from different sides by magpies. On its swaying branch the heavy cockatoo kept looking around and waiting for the next onslaught – and they would swoop in from different directions, at the same time.

Photography: posterity (almost).

On her birthday he said to her, 'I never thought I'd sleep with an 80-year-old woman.'
    He was 92.

'"If thou wouldst know contentment, let thy deeds be few," said the sage. Better still, limit them strictly to such as are essential, and to such as in a social being reason demands, and as it demands. This brings about contentment that comes of doing a few things and doing them well. Most of what we say and do is not necessary, and its omission would save both time and trouble. At every step, therefore, a man should ask himself, "Is this one of the things that are super-fluous?" Moreover, not idle actions but even idle impressions ought to be suppressed; for then unnecessary action will not ensue.'

— Aurelius

Unoriginal minds are opposed to 'generalisa-tions', and are quick to say so.

A general nearness (to another person).

More men would be misanthropic if they had distinctive ideas.

'Have you ever watched those American cooking shows? They still do garnishes.' Two women in café (loud).

William McDonald in jail 34 years, killed 4 men. 'I have tried so many times to associate with people . . . And each time I tried, I developed lower self-esteem. My life improved since I came to jail. In jail I have got the stability and I don't have to relate to people.

'The trouble is to take things too seriously. I am highly strung. It makes life harder. I don't think that life is funny at all.'

The racket of wings taking off was merely someone landing in a puddle.

Man delivering mattress. He said, 'It's four years today since my best mate was electrocuted. He was standing in water, reached up to a pipe and it cooked him. Three beautiful kids . . . And get this. His wife had a baby with the policeman that found him. What d'you make of *that*?'

To her, flowers are what are beautiful; flowers are 'beauty'. So she brings them, a reflex action, indoors onto curtains, cushions, footstools, shower curtains and shower caps, on the towels (and on the tea-towels), framed as prints on the wall, printed on rubbish bins, on the bread bin, on tiles, the coffee mugs and toilet paper, and finally on her dresses.

'"But having more of a life is one of the earliest and subtlest signs of mediocrity," Ulrich thought.'

A case of not knowing whether this is fiction, or Musil's own opinion.

As men grow older they speak less and search for words as if speaking a second language.

Theatre: applauding commonplaces.

Gericault's teacher told him his paintings resembled nature the way a violin case resembles a violin.

Still angry, the Englishwoman, remembering her husband, a Spitfire pilot killed after they had been married only six weeks. The coffin they sent back to her filled with nothing but mud.

Canetti soaks up personalities and their ideas like a sponge and squeezes out a belief.

Magpie warbling in the park like water bubbling out of a pipe.

While talking to her sister on the phone she casually inspects her various body blemishes.

Book concerning English religious wisdom cited by Ruskin, *Natural History of Enthusiasm*.

To display a sort of humbleness she chose modest cardigans, etc. which actually drew attention to her humbleness.

'There is nothing certain except that nothing is certain, and nothing more wretched than Man nor more arrogant.'
                                        – Pliny (inscribed on ceiling in
                                            Montaigne's library)

'You sound like my father.' Young women use the spectre of their fathers as a convenient parking spot for the more difficult feelings.

Two women on seawall: 'I need to have a non-intense relationship.' 'Yes, that always helps.'

'His name was – what was his name? It was the name of an English town.'

His nose drew attention to itself. Speaking, he expanded and twisted his nostrils, a fastidious sniffing. Originally it may have expressed distaste. Now it animated his face whatever he said.

'X-rays on a 62-year-old Brazilian woman who complained of slight stomach pains found she was in fact carrying the skeleton of a foetus conceived outside her womb up to fifteen years ago, a surgeon said yesterday.' – *Australian*, 3.4.96

His sister was called Norma Carless.

Life expectancy in England was 40 in 1583.

They wore large brown boots, thick knitted pullovers, and happily spoke all night about wood-burning stoves.

Near Gundaroo. Early morning mist really was like a snake leaving the valley.

All night the primordial bellowing of cows distraught at having their heifers taken from them.

He was 'profoundly unmarried'.

Early in the morning the woman in the basement flat coughs like a vomiting cat.

'That's so depressing I'm going to buy myself a cake.' Man at interval during *A Cheery Soul*.

Eyes the colour of cognac. Surely it has been said before.

Colossal Russian Orthodox priest with hair tied in a pony tail, long wispy beard. And two female admirers from his congregation, one rather gaunt. The strange sexual attraction of certain priests, often of the large bodied ones (even more unattainable).

Surprising how noisy a single tree can be (wind in the Flinders Ranges).
   Around Wilpena the colours are naturally *ours*: silver-greys, pale browns. The pink of galahs.

Aunt J., aged 84, widowed, gazed away when my mother vomited and collapsed in the restaurant on her 80th, as if thinking: I too am at the end of my life, and this is what it is like. It was women who rushed about helping my mother, men standing back, 'in case they were needed'. Here again, women suffer less from public embarrassment.

Anubis, the barking god.

'When collating objects no quality is so universal as diversity and variety.'          – Montaigne

Above all is Montaigne's worldliness. It is earned; and he assumes it. Whereas Stendhal, worldly too, prizes it, wears it almost too languidly.

Two solicitors at the Trustee company and their stories about their clients.

– Man left large sum to his wife on condition she remarried, so that 'someone else can see what an unpleasant, mean and selfish bitch she was'.

– Man with sizeable estate and instructions to give it all to the Australian Government: 'I don't have anybody else.'

– Woman who won two lotteries and kept $1.5 million in a savings account. All was bequeathed to about a dozen people who gradually died until a woman in Adelaide received the lot.

– The philosopher in the shearing shed. Masses of papers. He wanted his 'philosophy' published.

'He imported a wife from South America.'

'Octave was happier, and became more intelligent.'
                                    – Stendhal, *Amance*

Someone was talking about the sensuality of treachery.

A refined sort of man, but so hectic he was often uncouth.

You're here briefly – work, give shape.

Fat man at the concert sat with legs splayed, overflowing onto my seat, his warmth flowed into me. His body felt warmer than mine. As a consequence I felt he knew more about most things than me.

The fat man as know-all – common?

Chinese general during the Cultural Revolution who married the wife of the man he jailed for twenty years.

'Lack of moderation (in art) exposes to view the producer of art, and for that reason destroys the illusion that I am not perceiving it, but creating it.'                                    – Tolstoy, *Journals*

I think about death with greater composure than I think about certain people.

At R.H.'s funeral service the embroidered pew cushions on either side: Dora Heron 1847–1907, Jean M. Snowball, 1899–1964. Noticed R.'s nose repeated in his brother, and his gaunt mother.

Melbourne debutante's dress flown out from Paris in diplomatic bag. That was years ago.

What attracted her to the engineer who answered her lonely hearts advertisement was the stamped, self-addressed envelope he enclosed. After ten minutes of their first meeting she rested her head on his shoulder.

The wife of a lighthouse keeper who became addicted to kite-flying.

'A thesaurus of menace.'

She was incapable of sitting on a chair; it had to be the floor.

B. told with a certain relish of a Russian he'd met in Prague, an ex-monk who, after being harsh with women, would slash his face with a razor.
    His face crisscrossed, multiplying the torment.

The metronomic movement of masts in Rush-cutter's Bay: can musical intervals be related to tides?

25.5.97. Red in the face, and feel as if someone is choking me.

The excruciating interior furnishings of musicians.

'Novels arise out of the shortcomings of history.'

R.F. told of her father, the meteorologist, a specialist in ice movement and continental drift. He was a Jew in Berlin, in the 30s. In 1931 he went on an expedition towards the North Pole. They became trapped. He caught frostbite; his toes were removed with a can opener. One German set out for the base with an Eskimo. He was found a year later in his tent, dead. The Eskimo was never seen again. The three others stayed in the ice cave, mostly in sleeping bags through the winter.

Back in Berlin, he was appointed Meteorological Officer for Germany. In 1934 he spoke out privately against the Nazis, and was betrayed by one of the two men who had shared the ordeal in the ice cave (though not the one who had cut off his toes). He spent six months in prison; released after the intervention of Hess's father. In Cambridge he worked at the Polar Research Centre. He would visit Wittgenstein in his bare rooms. 'You don't have many books.' There were none. W.: 'I'm here to think, not to read.'

People warned him not to return to Germany. But as he was about to return it was announced that no Jews could hold public office etc. He was offered Head of Meteorology in Argentina, Egypt and Australia. He arrived in Melbourne in 1937, recommended by Mawson. He went several times to Antarctica.

Without toes he shuffled around Melb. University campus like a drunk; wore out his shoes at odd angles.

'Woman, outside of love, is boring, although she doesn't know it.'                                          – Camus

R.'s great-grandfather, a widower in Bendigo, made a fortune on the gold fields. At 60, he was having affairs with two sisters in their twenties. Eventually he said he'd marry the first one who became pregnant. He then had six children by the one he married. Did he prefer the other sister, who didn't get pregnant?

On both voyages I noticed the crew became cheerful approaching a port. But then they became cheerful again leaving the port, heading out to sea.

Her love is uneven, even her generosity is uneven; so that when she is generous she makes too much of it to herself, privately.

Man lying dead outside McDonald's, Kings Cross. Early forties, overweight. During the heart attack he pissed his pants: lay on his back on the footpath, arms outstretched, shirt torn open by ambulance men, his face grey. A crowd of about thirty waited, mouths open, for him to show signs of life. A death without any dignity at all.

'Capitalism without bankruptcies is like Christianity without Hell.'

I feel like a fox cornered in a cave, a fox with poor eyesight. Jan. 1998.

'. . . Women get angry only to make us angry in turn, imitating the laws of love.'   – Montaigne

Am surrounded by good people, decent people; only occasionally am I decent.

English pianist, thin, pale, protruding teeth who flung one arm in the air each time she finished a sonata, the way famous people used to turn and wave before stepping into aeroplanes.

Hot foreign places seem to produce homesickness.

He removes the bones of fish (for her).

As you can see, I'm not very good at this – whatever this is.

Girl to another (earnestly): 'My skin's dehydrated, but it's not dry.'

'Real superiority . . . admits no eccentricity.'
— Delacroix, *Journals*

In the Freud Museum, Vienna
  '. . . I too have had my spitting headaches and attacks of fatigue like anyone else, that I was a passionate smoker (I wish I still were), that I ascribe to the cigar the greatest share of my self-control and tenacity in work . . .'
— letter to Stefan Zweig

A visitor to the museum stole one of Freud's hats hanging on the original hat stand. The thief's analyst told him to return it. Freud's hats, coat and walking stick are now behind a perspex cover.

In Freud's house in London, the cavern-like quality of his consulting room, the heavy drapes, brown-stained wood, the masses of small sculptures arranged on his desk, and the couch, all added to the mystery, the bearded shaman figure dispensing cures and predictions to the tribe.

Cistercian monastery, le Thoronet. Beelike humming of tourists. It was the acoustics.

His habit of kissing his wife's head solemnly, almost too solemnly.

On the container ship in the Red Sea the Third Officer said his father, near Munich, had the contract in the 1930s and throughout the war to make picture frames – to hold Hitler's photograph in all the Town Halls, railway stations, government offices etc. of Germany.

'. . . just as there are certain women whose age you cannot guess, there was no way to tell what time it was.'          – Kadare, *Broken April*

For exercise, Bismarck in his lifetime cut down 30,000 trees.

As the body fell (from 10,000 or more feet) he knew there was no hope of surviving so he inspected his fingernails.

How much of it is love; how much merely avoiding the horror?

At home (London) the German editor in slippers pulled out his pipe and told how he had only recently the first time met his father, a priest, and he too had been wearing the same leather slippers, smoking a pipe, had the same kind of books, and was singing in another room the same song he himself often sang. According to the editor's wife they also stood with legs apart in a similar manner. She, opinionated, talkative, plump and complacent, from NZ.

Men usually do not mind, yet women dislike to be told they look like another woman.

To be close to somebody it is obviously necessary for conversation to continue – with ease and freedom. Instead and now: nausea at odd times etc., from the loss.

J. listens to others and thinks she is expressing her own feelings. So her inconsistency.

To be kicked by a dead horse.

Baby crying like a seagull.

'There is no greater sorrow than thinking back upon a happy time in misery.'
— *Inferno*, Canto 5

Sheep and cattle condemned to eat all day, sheep especially.

15.10.98. The sun would be streaming in through the window at Bellevue Hill. Outside there is light, shadows, rooftops and green – and a street sloping up to the sea.

In our country people die of thirst. A beginning.

M.D. had the ashes of her mother in a jar in the cupboard. When she went into hospital for an operation she asked – if she didn't survive – a friend to mix her ashes with her mother's. The friend immediately phoned around all her friends, telling them.

How to be a good person, while at the same time preserving – and increasing – one's individuality. The problem of any artist, especially ordinary ones.

Unable to bear the emotions aggravated by music; so haven't listened.

'Young Mr Dupret shouted to himself.'

In Bondi after the war there was a bin or bucket placed by a charity filled with false teeth. People could try them and, if they fitted, take them to wear without cost.

C. So mournful, so ostentatiously modest. Striving in that way for superiority.

Without fail whenever I pass St Luke's in Roslyn Gardens, where I saw the snake three years ago, I remember it.

'Does awareness of another's faults constitute talent?'  — Stendhal, *H. Brulard*

How I exaggerate illness – there is blood, but not much; and how others like it exaggerated, helping them to help me.

There's a great mass of literary politeness, of faintly skimming the psychological surface. Nothing more.

Large areas of my life, as I have formed it, have been altered and whole areas destroyed. Old friends have turned away or look at me differently.

In every life the unexpected has the power of deflection etc. – out of all proportion; in the novel too (Stendhal, Tolstoy, Tournier etc.), it gives energy, increases curiosity, alertness, and so moves the novel closer to 'life'.

The thirsty cries of sheep. Outside Canberra.

'I would make a gloomy wife,' she said. But she was already married.

8.3.99. In the past ten years I have become more complex. It has made me more interesting, and yet less attractive.

G. booked a room in the Hotel Carlton in Brisbane, once the offices of the Lands Department, to spend a weekend with a married woman from Melbourne. He discovered the room had originally been his father's office – now fitted with double bed, bathroom etc. 'It made the weekend difficult.'

B. Palace. Queen sat in a small room full of dark Dutch paintings. The Governor of Victoria had visited earlier in the morning. 'Did I know him?' She asked if I used a computer. 'No, no, no,' I shook my head. To avoid sounding troglodyte, I quickly said, 'But if Dickens were alive today he'd be the first to use one.' To this she replied in her slightly high voice, 'Then we'd have even more of his books.'

The hollow grandeur of a palace: it must not resemble an ordinary house. The over-scale of everything, the width of the stairs, long, long corridors, sofas that could safely seat ten along walls. Overall a certain vulgarity. Yards and yards of paintings, each painting rendered equally replaceable, even the Vermeer I stopped before and examined. The exaggeratedly casual *aide-de-camp*, in RAF uniform, kept glancing at my name on a tiny piece of paper in the palm of his hand. Neither he nor the lady-in-waiting, who chatted like a sparrow, knew there was no Turner in the Royal collection.

American aid worker at breakfast said he was 'the happiest man alive. I wake up every morning happy.' Fifteen years ago he gave away all his money, about $15 million, and now travels the world arranging donations of pharmaceuticals to the poorest countries. He locks in eye contact, and with it a belief in himself and his task. His salesmanship, his rapid factual delivery was similar to any travelling American salesmen of the mid-west kind, although here for entirely different purposes.

Stendhal's advice to his sister: 'Remind yourself, above all, of this great and immutable truth: all men are cold, mediocre and love to hurt those they believe to be happy.'

P.'s brother-in-law in Brisbane had one eye missing and would never say how he lost it.

'I never saw green grass for the first 17 years of my life.'

He invented a cough.

The importance of resistance: without it the viewer, or the reader, hardly contributes. Going from Cézannes to the roomful of Cossington Smiths – resistance was what was missing. After Mallarmé, Valéry 'could no longer suffer impure poems, which could be understood at once and without resistance. Everything seemed naïve and slack after they had read him.'

Woman was raped in Sydney, aged 19, and had a daughter from it. Daughter fostered out. Mother moved to Brisbane where she married. Eighteen years later the daughter asked for mother's identification; writes; is invited to Brisbane. The mother's husband sees his wife in the girl's features. They have intense affair. Mother finds out. Daughter returns to Sydney. Man and woman continue living in Brisbane.

We are a strange 'people' to have nailed a person, or persons, on a cross.

16.10.99. At Beare Park, grey Saturday, reading and smoking: looked up to see black container ship sliding out between yachts, out on its voyage, and felt pang of envy – to be back on board such a steel ship, facing the ocean and different weathers.

Sheep in distant paddocks moving slowly like maggots.

The way the two old men talk eagerly on their morning walk indicates they have known each other only recently.

'What a deale of cold business doth a man mis-spend the better part of life in! in scattering *complements*, tendering *visits*, gathering and venting *newes*, following *Feasts* and *Playes*, making a little winter-love in a darke corner.'

– Jonson

When coming to rest in an avalanche, dribble to see which way is up.

All the death, or rather, the rows of dying at the hospice; lying patiently waiting; and I feel I'm not changed by it. Faint feeling of superiority towards others outside on the footpath.

During the war two sisters on Salisbury railway station stood next to a big man, a soldier, to shelter from cold wind. He was an Australian. It was how she met her husband, a farmer from semi-desert country.

Does the man who laughs uncontrollably have an argument with himself?

At concerts women bowed to his father, the surgeon. Later he explained that they were women whose breasts he had removed.

Everything's temporary, in stages.

Woman in South Africa called her son Richard. Because she wanted him to be rich and hard. And that is what he became.

Explaining her husband: 'He is much more intimate on the telephone.'

* * *

Madrid. On the narrow footpaths people step aside so often to allow another to pass they do not expect thanks or give thanks themselves. It produces a frank expressionless manner in other aspects of daily life. Priest smoking a cigar on the street, then a few minutes later another one. Why not? Small shops displaying ochre underwear for old maids. Men with hands in their pockets appraising pistols in gun shop window. Naturally pistols attract more attention than the shotguns and the rifles.

Unaccustomed items on menu: cold vegetable soup, chicken with fish . . .

Here the hotel doormen resemble out-of-work admirals, field marshals and generals.

Catholic country: young man begging on the street by crouching on knees with arms outstretched in medieval supplication posture.

She said Cortazar died of a rare disease: everything kept growing.

Literature – old deep stories – written in the faces. All demanding to be made stories of. These are Spanish faces on the street, fleshy and deeply lined.

On the street here the woman takes the man's arm. There are few exceptions among the older people; a national habit has formed. Younger couples and even many older couples walk along holding hands. Some time ago there was little of this. Gradually a critical mass of social habit developed, until so many women were taking the man's arm or couples were walking hand-in-hand that anyone who didn't forced a question on themselves, on their public feelings for each other, since they were exposed by the majority.

Beatrix, in Barcelona, and her father: he disapproved of the men her sister had. He'd tear open her letters to inspect the photographs. 'He looks like an idiot. Look how hairy. Is he some sort of ape or what?' Etc. The man she eventually settled for owned a furniture store, and as a gesture of goodwill the father bought a lounge suite, but could barely bring himself to sit on the chairs, complaining about their quality etc.

Both free and narrowing to be in a strange city without someone intimate nearby to make observations to, and weigh up those observations.

And German paintings (Stuttgart) heavy-handed like German cuisine and German room-service.

A novel that . . . To write a novel which . . . Etc., etc.

Hurling themselves at each other always, some-where, like ants.

F.'s last conversation with the painter J.B. was ... about braces. B. thought that instead of wearing a belt F.W. would look better wearing braces.

Try looking down, as if above the streets and the crowds.

As a young girl in the 1940s she worked in a flower shop in Nice, and sold flowers to Matisse. 'He would come in, always correct. He always asked if we had anything special. He wanted flowers out of the ordinary.' She also sold Matisse unusual fruits and vegetables – pine-apples, eggplants etc. – which he used in his paintings. A small unsmiling French woman, with a deep voice. Now in her 80s, dying in a hospice in Sydney.

'Anyone who turns his prime attention on to himself will hardly ever find himself in the same state twice. I give my soul this face or that, depending on which side I lay down on. I speak about myself in diverse ways: that is because

I look after myself in diverse ways. Every sort of contradiction can be found in me: timid, insolent, chaste, lecherous: talkative, taciturn: tough, sickly: clever, dull, brooding, affable; lying, truthful: learned, ignorant; generous, miserly and then prodigal – I can see something of all that in myself . . .'          – Montaigne

Her Australian wrists, Australian arms.

Here they are calling meat pies 'rat coffins'.

'I prefer the telescope to the microscope as a working tool. But because I had the misfortune to begin a book with the word "I", people jumped to the conclusion that, instead of seeking to uncover laws in general, I was undertaking "self-analysis", in its most personal and detestable sense.'          – Proust

Man asleep in park with hand in dog's mouth.

Soft drops of rain encouraged the leaves of the frangipani to loosen and fall – which was enough to see nature gently at work.

Loud woman in bank (Kings Cross) asking for a loan: 'I have a grand piano, I have artworks.'


'Never bolt your door with a boiled carrot.'


Begin: 'At 51, when he should have known better . . .'


He has lived alone for so long – over a year – his way of talking had become a blurting, an abruptness, bluntness, that even to him began to sound interesting.


She was like water; no shape, no opinions. He felt he could pass his hands through her.


'There was not much point in trying to catch a falling piano' – Wall Street broker explaining fall in the market.


Alone in the apartment, and then meeting people, I feel vague, floating, without focus. In body and mind, drifting; slowly reaching a natural level, natural definition.

A mother reassuring 60-year-old son: 'You don't look like a fat man.'

A man in Sydney whose name is Stanley Livingstone.

P.N.'s father during the war walking down narrow street in Darlinghurst at night unable to find (or afford) hotel; saw bed in basement – light on, door open. He went in and lay down. A young woman appeared in the door: 'What are you doing here?' He patted the bed beside him, 'Come and lie down.' She did. They eventually married (happily).

It makes no difference whether literature is European, American, British, or Australian, as long as it allows me to enter and contemplate. Prefer inventions, those that more or less reach the area of myth (the broadest sense). Kadare, Tournier, Marguerite Yourcenar etc.; *Madame Bovary* – 'myth'. *The Illiad*. Little interest in literature – or painting, music – produced merely for *effect*. The confessional, self-analysis in the first person which is now common: it's difficult, though not impossible, for it to enter 'myth'.

For five years this Sydney man had been a bull-fighter in Spain, now a solicitor married with children. He never told his family. Only when they visited Spain and he was recognised by people on the street did he tell them.

Two women walking in park early in morning. One speaking earnestly: 'She's the sort of woman who has three friends and doesn't need any other.'

'I have the awful problem now of being a better person before I can paint better.' — C. McCahon

Mitterand, asked what quality is most required in a leader: 'Indifference.'

B. was nine months old in 1944 when his father died in a Lancaster bomber over Germany. His mother never remarried. Her recurring dream was hearing a knock on the door and opening it as an old woman to find her pilot-husband there, a 21-year-old man. She died at 58.

Ernst Junger noted as 'curious' that in the extreme circumstances of the trenches other people remain the most popular subject for conversation.

M.D. has died. When we first met more than 20 years ago, she listened to every word I said; later she would argue with me; finally – for the longest period – she took no notice of anything I said. I liked all those stages. I often wanted to see her. Even her generosity was distinctive.

More and more I am pleased to be the second born. I was born happier, I have given myself *charm*.

From train (near Woy Woy): old turquoise-coloured barge rotting in khaki water. Man opposite, asleep, smelling like a wet dog.

Chinese man learning English with polite acquaintance, '"Generally" – please, what does that mean?'

'She suffered from absolute isolation which, I suspected, was related to self-absorption.'

Migrant woman at language course, when asked to write a sentence, wrote: 'I am a burden to my daughter.'

'You see, dearest, I always knew, even as a kid, that I could only exist in love. And that is why I was so frightened that I might simply get lost. And so I made myself independent . . . And when I met you, suddenly I was no longer afraid . . . It still seems incredible to me that I managed to get both things – the "love of my life" and a oneness with my self. And yet, I only got the one thing when I got the other. But finally I also know what happiness is.'

– Hannah Arendt, to her husband

High Commissioner's wife. She met him, she said, while sunbathing on a wall in Portugal. He was looking for her friend. She got up and walked ahead of him. 'There's a fat Englishman here, who's just your type.' Months later at a dinner in London her long hair caught fire as she bent over the table. It was he who appeared at her elbow and put out the flames.

Flaubert's unrestrained, rather brutal views ('I curse women: they are the cause of all our woes' etc.) to Georges Sand, and her tolerant, all too decent protests in reply. And it is Flaubert, who remains the stronger, more distinctive over time.

This attraction to music is spreading insistently, but not in every direction, and it only goes so far. I am a surface listener, dutifully waiting to go deeper.

All around were hills and valleys, about waist high. The sea was busily mimicking land. It was a charcoal expanse, desolate, streaked with lines of quartz, the way a land is left after fire. Each miniature hill and following valley replaced another. Lines of quartz there dissolved into trails of lace. It was the sea, said to be soothing.

Since she has died I think only occasionally of mother, perhaps because she remains part of me.

'. . . intelligence and goodness – what more can one want in a human being?'        – Milosz

Has a small reddish face; when her hair is pulled back it reveals her teeth, sending them forward. Likes to say, 'I'm boring, but that's all right.'

When he was very young, G. learnt his father didn't like him – not at all. It made him unable to trust, etc. He went through life not properly equipped, out of balance.

Everything I do is difficult. Writing, reading, talking, not talking, walking, loving.

Started his laugh loudly which went down at the end to a sort of practised hiccuping. It became a laugh about laughing itself. A deliberately friendly man.

The laugh is manufactured to attract attention. By loudly – and visually, in the extreme – acknowledging a thing just said the laugh smothers and neutralises it.

The main enterprise in the world. Enterprise – a good word.

Whereas the smile is mostly signal.

Knowledge of death makes us wish to extend our lives at the expense of others?

The entrails of myth crawl all over Europe, some-times bringing on forest-darkness, leaving in its wake fairytales, indelible opera plots, 'irrational' warlords. Without the underyling strength of myth, fiction may well be pleasant and interesting, and perhaps even topical, but lacking in deeper-depth, and so, portability.

Humour is superiority.

According to Schnabel he was 'attracted only to music which I consider to be better than it can be performed'. He didn't play Chopin, Debussy or Ravel. Also in his memoirs he tells of being attracted to the young singer who would become his wife. He saw her boots left to be cleaned outside her hotel room – the size of her feet.

Sitting slightly too close to the man with enormous hands.

Poisonous snakes have small heads.

There was that tremendous black sky over the dark river, and the dark forest on the far shore. The Rajang at Sibu.

By then my face was aching from trying to understand.


Kindness closely associated with loneliness.


The paint chosen for the bookshelves here happened to be named on the paint chart 'Simone Weil Grey'. And so not an ordinary matt grey – it could be industrial.


Caption to photograph: 'Churchill, the brick-layer.'


Brushing P.P.'s hair a few days before she died. Her head scarcely out of the sheet. It was shrunken, her recognisable features – nose, small eyes – had become exaggerated. Keeping her eyes closed she smiled. Even then and with little hair she could acknowledge pleasure.


Forced to feel these feelings.


M.'s dark-haired cousin from Christchurch had recently divorced; on her visit to Sydney it was up to M. to entertain her. They decided to go to discotheques to pick up men. They went to three or four; sat around, watched and drank. They had no luck with men. At 2am on the footpath M. suddenly confessed, 'I'm a whore.' She said it as a joke, to liven things up. But her cousin threw her arms around her and admitted, 'So am I.' And almost wept.

Surely it is true of anybody: now and then I don't feel I exist at all. This happened twenty minutes ago.

Mouth – perfect as a surname.

By then my face was aching from trying to understand.

Much to be learnt from Wagner's deliberate withholding – at crucial moments in *Tristan*, *Lohengrin*, etc. – although its origins are in the sexual act.

Man who could imitate a telephone ringing. Three hundred years ago it would have been clock chimes or a cart creaking.

Apart from that the golden rule of monarchs appears to be: move slowly.

She is so happy she takes no notice of him.

Time is compressed for the traveller?

There is the firm instinct for a man to discuss his wife as little as possible.

Love between two people can never be equal.

It is only a matter of time in a Russian novel before a sturgeon arrives on a plate, a 'fine sturgeon' or a 'large sturgeon'. It is like the appearance of bicycles in Irish novels. The sturgeon makes its appearance on a plate held by an old footman in a greasy shirt. Other times a landlord of an inn brings the fish half cold to a filthy table. At a rundown estate a traveller is ushered into the presence of the impoverished landowner, tucking into a local sturgeon (Gogol). Russian characters have healthy appetites. They've been travelling on bad roads, in badly sprung carriages.

Where else in literature do you find a languid

landowner pondering a pleasantly wasted life, while at the same time reaching out, as if for another slice of sturgeon, for some essential, life-saving truth?

As the world grows larger more and more people will want to draw attention to themselves.

In *Youth* Tolstoy writes, 'Again the Princess smiled her unnatural, yet characteristically natural, smile.'

'For forms of government let fools contest.'
— Pope

There was always competition to see who could become the worst soldiers.

Farmer near Armidale. His grandfather fought Germans in the First World War. He returned to farm, hating them. A young German wool buyer arrived; the farmer could hardly do business with him – could barely talk to him. The German fell for his daughter. But then he was interned during the Second World War. Daughter was patient. In 1946 they were married. They lived in one side of the grandfather's homestead and managed one side of the property, each side not speaking. A house divided like Berlin. Only the dogs crossed the divide. During the day the German's dogs preferred the other side. When he died, the German left his side of the property to the other side, as is the custom in rural districts.

'Love is of all the sentiments the most egoistic, and, as a consequence, when it is wounded, the least generous.'                                   – B. Constant

He hurt her by getting too close to her or not close enough.

The leaves looked dusty in the headlights.

I went to India to see dead people.

In Amsterdam the streets are the long gangways, water just below, on one side. The buildings form the ship's infrastructure, windows looking onto the water. Large pulleys fitted to the gables of buildings to allow cargo to be lifted on board. And inside, the houses have steep narrow staircases with handrails, also like an old ship.

'Timewise, it took quite a few days.'

What man can be a bungler throughout his working life and still be respected? Clergyman.

Man (in Provence) tells younger swimmer she cannot land on his property. Exhausted, she falls back into water. He then allows her to land, giving his hand. They have an affair for two years; children. His wife, owner of the house where it all began, left him.

Seven deaths in the life of a writer.

On the phone considering a friend's suffering from difficulties with a man, she sounded very similar to someone supervising a film script.

R. in P.A. hospital two days before he died. Restless, agitated. 'Nothing means anything.' And to me, 'You have lost your way. I'm sorry, but I think you have.'

Visiting Crete in his twenties, E.'s father saw a photo of a young woman in window of photographer's studio. Photographed because she was beautiful. He asked who she was. The photographer gave her name and the village. People there directed him to the house. He asked her to marry him. She was in love with a man in the village, but the man's brother had 'something wrong in the head'; so the parents instructed her to marry the bold stranger. Two children were born. Never really happy.

Mozart's *Requiem*, St Augustin, Vienna. The conductor, scarcely 40, balding, opened his mouth wide and glared at parts of the choir like the rabid monkey on that path outside Delhi in 1969. One singer, top row, wore a black raincoat.

> *If he who I wait for*
> *Should come now, what will I do?*
> *This morning the snow-covered garden*
> *Is so beautiful without a trace of footprints.*
> — Poem by Japanese woman a thousand
> years ago; Izumi Shikibu (974–1034)

Her father was a mushroom farmer in England. After he died unexpectedly, she took to eating mushrooms (on toast) every lunchtime. She 'loved' mushrooms.

The dentist said 'thankyou' to his assistant so many times every day that she began to despise him.

According to Walter Benjamin, a Strasbourg piano-maker, Schmidt, made the first guillotine.

*The Bathers.* After stepping back and surveying his life, the way an artist's work is displayed in rooms of different sizes, R.H. saw only misunderstandings and misery he had caused or suffered, and decided to change his ways. He was forty-eight. For the remaining years he wanted peace and quiet. He was not interested in complications. Most of his recent difficulties with people had been incomprehensible to him. And yet clearly there were aspects of his personality which produced strong reactions in others, though what these were he was not sure. From now on he was going to avoid complications. He would make himself as small as possible. The course of action was to sell up and move to another state, to a place entirely out of character, and live alone quietly. A life of conscious quietness! People would hardly know he was breathing. He would keep to himself. It would be an anonymous life. The fewer people he had contact with, the fewer the complications. When he looked back over the years he realised that he had talked too much. It was words which had caused the difficulties, nothing else. Settling down in strange surroundings, where he knew nobody, he would keep words to a minimum. If people wanted to say things about him they would have precious little to work with. From now on R.H. would open his mouth as little as possible. This would also give him clarity. He wanted serenity. As a consequence he could devote himself to his studies and thoughts in general, without becoming involved with anyone else. Above all – and this he decided with a grim expression, while shaving – he would keep well clear of—

A face troubled with kindness.

Looking down at my fingers and hands I am often amazed – that they work, appear to have a purpose.

To be modest without resorting to secrecy.

How S.'s prissy aversion to vomit, especially in literature, has produced the very opposite to what such 'refinement' intended – an overbearing provincialism.

During an argument she hurled the jewellery he had given her out the window; pieces landed over a wall in a nunnery where he had to search around for them, appearing to her as a miserly man.

The traveller who collects countries and shows them to others like extremely rare postage stamps.

'Every man who dies resembles the man that survives and asks him to account for it.'

– Pavese

Draped on a desk in the living room were the war medals of C.'s grandfather. The VC plain and as heavy and as dark as cast iron: 'FOR VALOUR.' Nevertheless possessed an unmistakeable, silent power.

For ten years Ciorian corresponded with a Japanese admirer. Then she announced she was coming to Paris. Alarmed, he asked K. who was going to Tokyo to check her out. In Tokyo, K. left a message for the woman, but changed to a more comfortable hotel, without telling the woman. They never met. In Paris, Ciorian refused to speak to K. Whenever he saw her, he crossed the street.

Husband greeting wife was like this: in shirt sleeves, he took her elbow and leaned on her. Then stepped back.

Iceland, 6.9.03. Covered in moss like seaweed left on a vast rocky beach. Hardly anywhere a tree. The only trees were silver birches in the capital, in gardens, shipped in from some other place. And rocks – large, significant boulders – have floated to the surface on public lawns and people's front gardens. The houses with their corrugated iron roofs and walls, and rust patches touched up as on ships; otherwise, to reduce the industrial look they are painted pale blue, yellow, rhubarb, and the main windows decorated with fretwork. Many houses are dated, 1914, 1893 etc. – which immediately makes you wonder when corrugated iron was invented.

A bride and groom checked into the Hotel Holt, the bride in full white dress and veil.

Later another white bride in the back of a wedding car – talking on a mobile phone.

Reykjavik, a dogless town. Until recently

they were banned. Woman: 'There are too many horses in Iceland, too many.'

Sprayed on a wall, 'GOD IS LONELY'.


'See her? She was Miss Universe in 1964.' A somewhat broad, smiling woman.


So accustomed to rain they'd never seen an umbrella.


Laxness' solution: the one book he would take on the desert island would be *The Well-tempered Clavier*.


The deserted whaling station. Clothing and equipment left on benches and shelves, on hooks, on desks, as if workers had dropped tools and left only yesterday. Frozen in time. And in the barren fiord. No vandalism, only the paint peeling from the corrugated iron walls.

A woman – an unusually tall woman – was murdered at the station by whalers. Her body was cut into pieces and put in barrels of salt water. This is why, the waiter with the tattoo explained, the whaling station is haunted.

Every day a rainbow. It's only another rainbow. Invariably they produce a feeling of optimism.

In a bare volcanic valley a tiny Lutheran church standing alone. Painted white, with a pointless gate. Inside, the walls, floors, pews all wood, simple, unpainted. Barely six paces long, and a ceiling so low the beams had protective strips of rubber along the edges. Behind the altar, an abstract painting: broad bold colours, a yellow arch, red and bottle-green swathes – an H. Hodgkin, though more spontaneous. This was painted by a local policeman who was also an artist.

The tiny building declared a simple, practical religion. There was a deliberate connection inside the building to the bare earth and sky outside the building.

Berlin, 19.9.03. Beggar making a speech in train. His friendly dog wanted to stay behind.

Heaviness in Germany, heavily covered, dense; in the German language, in the word-growth

of German philosophy, in their art and architecture, in the cuisine; even in the public and
private gardens, closely grown dark-greenery,
dense, little light penetrating – 'the dark of the
earth' – so that the German instinct for the clear
air of the mountains, of the *sublime*, was a return
to the lightness and wide-openness of nature,
unnecessary nearby in France, Italy.

The concerts, exhibitions, theatre, opera,
cabarets, street musicians, festivals of all kinds,
television and lectures in Berlin are offerings to
people – to occupy and fill spaces, to distract.
Anything to avoid the solitude of self, or so it
seems.

They bought a house built of small bricks at
Charlottenberg, outside Copenhagen, from an
Icelandic man – a large difficult man, who made
a living importing herrings from Iceland. A wife
lived with him. Next door was a philosopher of
religion, of comparative religion, and wife. They
never spoke to the Icelandic man. During the
war he was in the Nazi party. And he sold
herrings to the German army. Shortly after the
war the police came to take him away for collab-
orating. His 16-year-old son ran out to stop
them. He was shot and killed near the front gate.
Every day the mother visited his grave.

When the Icelandic man died the neighbours wrote to the widow and invited her to tea. She accepted.


'A play on words' – strange thing to say.


First the invention of glass, amazing enough, then the mirror, which is not.


He wore ankle boots the colour of dates.


He had a stammer, but only – they said – when he was 'serious'.


Managed to preserve their marriage by going dancing every Monday night, without fail.


The East European composer now living in Sydney said of other composers: 'Music is like farting. If it is yours it is always interesting, not offensive; but anyone else's you want to leave the room.'

Spent so much time in the X-ray department his left arm had withered.

Roadworker, and gravel-voiced.

Psychology and philosophy: too much of one, not enough of the other.

Young woman with a thin man in the train reading out headline in a magazine: 'Why be friends with a failure?'

In the Botanical Gardens the plump coloured flowers and fleshy leaves, and the branches going forward from their beds, are sobering evidence that other things are growing on earth as we are. We exist among the ordinary selfishness of plants.

It is almost impossible to live without vanity.

That hot afternoon in Zimbabwe, lined up by the soldiers against the boot of the Peugeot with the other three men. Instead of the feeling of foolish vulnerability I prefer to recall the heat and stillness, and the grey dust on the trees.

Music and shame. Here shame can be in the guise of optimism.

Victoria Street. Young woman's way of greeting another, 'Have you been gruesome?'

If in painting the face in profile is the easiest way to capture likeness, why not in literature? Not seen much in everyday life.

Men and women in the film industry seem to have a preference for wearing black – the way a doctor wears a white coat, or surveyor corduroy trousers. It is as if they are in a darkened theatre, their faces pale in the darkness, which continues when they walk outside.

The psychology of the collector – one who collects too many objects. His loneliness is displayed, filled in. And yet within the loneliness is happiness.

In the Land of Pain. All blurry, then tilting.

V. told of meeting in Thirroul in 1953 a barber who swore he had cut Lawrence's hair — couldn't help laughing.


There was a prayer mat on the floor in the back of the taxi. I had my feet on it.


No use saying: If only we could live longer, there is not enough time etc. The brevity of life is in the design; it applies to every one of us.